Tableau 10.0 Best Practices

Develop a deep understanding of Tableau 10.0 and get to know tricks to understand your data

Jenny Zhang

BIRMINGHAM - MUMBAI

Tableau 10.0 Best Practices

First published: December 2016

Production reference: 1091216

Published by Packt Publishing Ltd.
Livery Place
35 Livery Street
Birmingham
B3 2PB, UK.
ISBN 978-1-78646-009-7

www.packtpub.com

Credits

Author

Jenny Zhang

Reviewers

Ravi Ratanlal Mistry
Sneha Vijay

Commissioning Editor

Veena Pagare

Acquisition Editor

Vinay Argekar

Content Development Editor

Rahul Popat

Technical Editor

Danish Shaikh

Copy Editor

Manisha Sinha

Project Coordinator

Nidhi Joshi

Proofreader

Safis Editing

Indexer

Mariammal Chettiyar

Graphics

Disha Haria

Production Coordinator

Nilesh Mohite

About the Author

Jenny Zhang is a technology professional with 6+ years' experience of data and analytics and currently working at JW Plater as Business Analytics Manager. She is a data strategist and technologist, Tableau and Alteryx community advocate, blogger. She had a series of blog posts about Tableau best practices at `http://jennyxiaozhang.com/tag/tableau/`.

Jenny is also passion about Big data. She had a series of blog posts about Big Data, NoSQL, Spark, Hadoop, and Yarn at `http://jennyxiaozhang.com/category/big-data/`.

Personal Site: `www.jennyxiaozhang.com`

LinkedIn: `www.linkedin.com/in/jennyxiaozhang`

I would like to thank you all the people who helped me with this book. Thank you all those who read, offered comments and helped in the editing and design. I would like to show special gratitude to Siddhesh Salvi, Vinay Argekar, Milton Dsouza from Packt publishing for enabling me to publish this book.

About the Reviewers

Ravi Ratanlal Mistry is an avid technology enthusiast and loves learning new concepts as well as teaching others. He holds a bachelor's degree in Information Technology and is a self-taught programmer.

I would like to thank my family and friends for their ongoing support, especially my mother for always believing in me.

Sneha Vijay has a well-rounded consulting background in domains of Data and Analytics with specialization in Tableau. Having over 4 years of experience and successful track record in Consulting, Analytics, Building sophisticated reporting technologies, Data Mining and Tableau visualizations, she provide users with the ability to examine information and uncover hidden trends and anomalies. Currently, Sneha works at Deloitte US Consulting based out of Gurgaon, India. Sneha's passions are spending time with his family, swimming and enjoying music to the fullest.

She has previously reviewed *Tableau 10 Business Intelligence Cookbook* with Packt Publishing.

www.PacktPub.com

For support files and downloads related to your book, please visit www.PacktPub.com.

Did you know that Packt offers eBook versions of every book published, with PDF and ePub files available? You can upgrade to the eBook version at www.PacktPub.com and as a print book customer, you are entitled to a discount on the eBook copy. Get in touch with us at service@packtpub.com for more details.

At www.PacktPub.com, you can also read a collection of free technical articles, sign up for a range of free newsletters and receive exclusive discounts and offers on Packt books and eBooks.

https://www.packtpub.com/mapt

Get the most in-demand software skills with Mapt. Mapt gives you full access to all Packt books and video courses, as well as industry-leading tools to help you plan your personal development and advance your career.

Why subscribe?

- Fully searchable across every book published by Packt
- Copy and paste, print, and bookmark content
- On demand and accessible via a web browser

Table of Contents

Preface

Introduction

Tableau 10.0 Best Practices will give you the useful tips from Tableau masters learned from years of experience working with Tableau. The book will show you the exact steps required to solve complex real-life problems. Whether it is data blending or complex calculations, you can solve your problem with ease and confidence; no more searching for help doc or waiting for support. This book will help you make the most of Tableau and become a Tableau expert.

What this book covers

Chapter 1, *Data Extraction* , covers tips, tricks, best practices on create, upload, manage, refresh Tableau data extracts. This is the first important step to make your data available for analytics in Tableau.

Chapter 2, *Data Blending*, covers tips, tricks, and best Practices on how to blend different data together using data blending in Tableau, such as how to differentiate primary and secondary data sources, what the difference between data blending and join is, and when to use which.

Chapter 3, *Calculation/Parameter*, covers advanced use cases of calculation and parameter. For example, how to use Table Calculations and LOD calculations to solve complex business analytics problems, how to use Dynamic Parameters to bring flexibility and interactivity to end user in your visualizations.

Chapter 4, *Sort and Filter*, covers advanced use cases of sort and filter. We will learn different types of sort and filter, how to sort/filter by calculated fields, differences among filter, group, and set, and how to use cascading filter and dynamic set/filter.

Chapter 5, *Formatting*, covers advanced tips and tricks on dashboard formatting. You will learn how to format tooltips to tell compelling stories, how to format individual measure, such as Excel, how to format date and create reference lines, and how to use dashboard actions.

Chapter 6, *Visualization*, covers tips, tricks, and best Practices on how to create different types of visualizations, such as stacked bar charts, scatterplot, waffle chart, jitter chart, circle chart, Network Graph, Calendar heat-map, multiple small maps.

Chapter 7, *Dashboard*, covers tips on how to create advanced dashboards following the Zen of dashboard design. We will learn how to do a five-second test of your dashboard, how to navigate between dashboards, how to embed YouTube videos in your dashboard, and so on.

Chapter 8, *Performance*, covers tips, tricks, and best Practices on improving performance. For example, how to optimize your calculations and data extract, how to make the best use of blending and join.

Chapter 9, *Permission*, covers tips, tricks, and best Practices on setting permissions. You will learn the permission hierarchy in Tableau, how the permission is inherited, and the best practices of setting permissions for your organization.

Chapter 10, *New features in Tableau 10*, covers new features available in Tableau Desktop 10. You will learn about more data connections available in Tableau 10, how to do cross-data set filter, cross-database join, geo grouping, how to format an entire workbook, and how to design device-specific dashboards.

What you need for this book

- Tableau Desktop 10
- Tableau Online/Tableau Server

Who this book is for

You'll gain the most from this book if you have a basic to medium understanding of the various features available in Tableau: knowing how to use Tableau to connect to different data sources and create a variety of visualizations to analyze your data. This book will help you become a master in using Tableau. You'll find this book useful if you spend a lot of time conducting data analysis and creating reports with Tableau.

Conventions

In this book, you will find a number of text styles that distinguish between different kinds of information. Here are some examples of these styles and an explanation of their meaning.

Functions are shown in capital letters. Functions used in calculation, appear in the text like this: "Ordinal calculations such as INDEX(), FIRST(), LAST(), SIZE(), LOOKUP(), and RANK()".

Reader feedback

Feedback from our readers is always welcome. Let us know what you think about this book—what you liked or disliked. Reader feedback is important for us as it helps us develop titles that you will really get the most out of.

To send us general feedback, simply e-mail feedback@packtpub.com, and mention the book's title in the subject of your message.

If there is a topic that you have expertise in and you are interested in either writing or contributing to a book, see our author guide at www.packtpub.com/authors.

Customer support

Now that you are the proud owner of a Packt book, we have a number of things to help you to get the most from your purchase.

Downloading the example datasets

You can download the example dataset files for this book from your account at http://www.packtpub.com. If you purchased this book elsewhere, you can visit http://www.packtpub.com/support and register to have the files e-mailed directly to you.

You can download the dataset files by following these steps:

1. Log in or register to our website using your e-mail address and password.
2. Hover the mouse pointer on the **SUPPORT** tab at the top.
3. Click on **Code Downloads & Errata**.
4. Enter the name of the book in the **Search** box.
5. Select the book for which you're looking to download the code files.
6. Choose from the drop-down menu where you purchased this book from.
7. Click on **Code Download**.

Once the file is downloaded, please make sure that you unzip or extract the folder using the latest version of:

- WinRAR / 7-Zip for Windows
- Zipeg / iZip / UnRarX for Mac
- 7-Zip / PeaZip for Linux

The datasets for the book is also hosted on GitHub at `https://github.com/PacktPublishing/Tableau-10-Best-Practices`. We also have other datasets and code bundles from our rich catalog of books and videos available at `https://github.com/PacktPublishing/`. Check them out!

Errata

Although we have taken every care to ensure the accuracy of our content, mistakes do happen. If you find a mistake in one of our books—maybe a mistake in the text or the code—we would be grateful if you could report this to us. By doing so, you can save other readers from frustration and help us improve subsequent versions of this book. If you find any errata, please report them by visiting `http://www.packtpub.com/submit-errata`, selecting your book, clicking on the Errata Submission Form link, and entering the details of your errata. Once your errata are verified, your submission will be accepted and the errata will be uploaded to our website or added to any list of existing errata under the Errata section of that title.

To view the previously submitted errata, go to `https://www.packtpub.com/books/content/support` and enter the name of the book in the search field. The required information will appear under the Errata section.

Piracy

Piracy of copyrighted material on the Internet is an ongoing problem across all media. At Packt, we take the protection of our copyright and licenses very seriously. If you come across any illegal copies of our works in any form on the Internet, please provide us with the location address or website name immediately so that we can pursue a remedy.

Please contact us at `copyright@packtpub.com` with a link to the suspected pirated material.

We appreciate your help in protecting our authors and our ability to bring you valuable content.

Questions

If you have a problem with any aspect of this book, you can contact us at `questions@packtpub.com`, and we will do our best to address the problem.

1
Data Extraction

A lot of enterprises today use Tableau to extract data from a variety of data sources. Data extraction is the first and an important step to make your data available to analytics in Tableau.

In this chapter, we will cover the following:

- Different ways of creating Tableau data extracts
- Technical details of how a Tableau data extracts works
- Creating extracts with a large volume of data efficiently
- Uploading and managing Tableau data extract in Tableau online
- Refreshing Tableau data extracts
- Using the Tableau web connector to create data extracts

Different ways of creating Tableau data extracts

Tableau provides a few ways to create extracts.

Direct connect to original data sources

Creating an extract by connecting to the original data source (Databases/Salesforce/Google Analytics, and so on) will maintain the connection to the original data source. You can right-click on the extract to edit it and then refresh it from the original data source.

Duplicate of an extract

If you create a duplicate of an extract by right-clicking on the data extract and selecting **Duplicate**, it will create a new .tde file and still maintain the connection to the original data source. If you refresh the duplicated data extract, it will not refresh the original data extract that you created the duplicate from. I will show you with the following example:

1. I have a data extract created by connecting to salesforce and pulling the user table. I am duplicating the data extract by right-clicking on it and selecting **Duplicate**, as shown in the following screenshot:

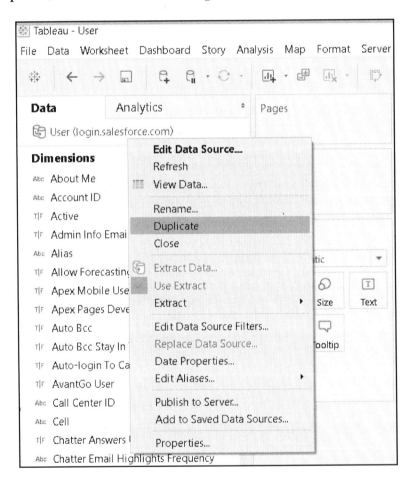

2. After duplicating the data extract, you will see that another data extract is created:

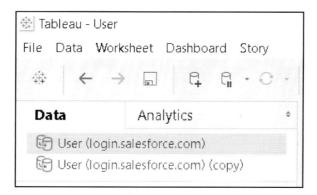

3. The refresh time for my original data extract is as follows:

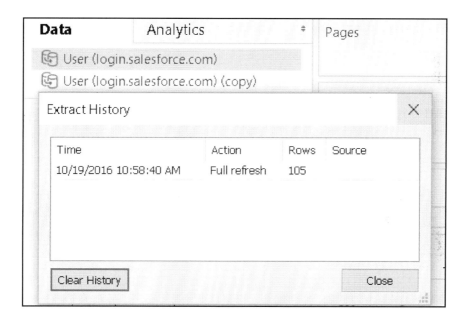

4. Then I refresh the duplicated data extract. The refresh time for my duplicated data extract is as follows:

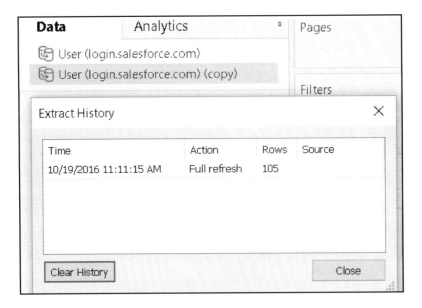

5. But when you check the refresh time for the original data extract, it is the same as before, as shown here:

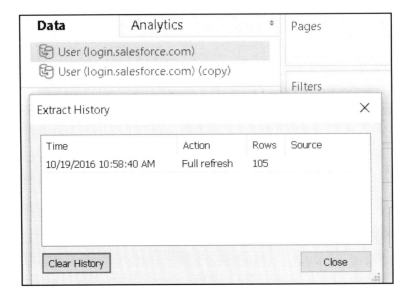

6. If you look at the data extract files, you can see that Tableau is creating another file for the duplicate:

Name	Date modified	Type
salesforce.1qhmboy0nne72f1dzgkey0g1c8kw_1vnmy8g08qf7v716hwgan0ue0tvu copy 1.tde	10/19/2016 11:11 ...	Tableau Extract
salesforce.1qhmboy0nne72f1dzgkey0g1c8kw_1vnmy8g08qf7v716hwgan0ue0tvu.tde	10/19/2016 10:59 ...	Tableau Extract

Connecting to a Tableau extract file

If you create a data extract by connecting to a Tableau extract file (.tde), you will not have that connection to the original data source that the extract is created from since you are just connecting to a local .tde file. You cannot edit or refresh the data from the original data source. Duplicating this extract by connecting to the local .tde file will not create a new .tde file. The duplication will still point to the same local .tde file.

You can right-click and select **Extract Data** to create an extract out of an extract. But we do not normally do that.

Technical details of how a Tableau data extract works

In the first section, we learn how to create data extract in Tableau. In order to further understand how data extract works and make the best use of it, let's learn about the technical details of how data extract works.

Tableau data extract's design principle

A Tableau extract (.tde) file is a compressed snapshot of data extracted from a large variety of original data sources (Excel, databases, Salesforce, NoSQL and so on). It is stored on disk and loaded into memory as required to create a Tableau visualization.

There are two design principles of the Tableau extract that make it ideal for data analytics.

- The first principle is that Tableau extract is a columnar store. The columnar databases store column values rather than row values. The benefit is that the input/output time required to access/aggregate the values in a column is significantly reduced. This is why Tableau extract is great for data analytics.

- The second principle is about how a Tableau extract is structured to make sure it makes the best use of your computer's memory. This will impact how it is loaded into memory and used by Tableau. To understand this principle better, we need to understand how Tableau extract is created and used as the data source to create visualization.

When Tableau creates data extract, it defines the structure of the .tde file and creates separate files for each column in the original data source. When Tableau retrieves data from the original data source, it sorts, compresses, and adds the values for each column to their own file. After that, individual column files are combined with metadata to form a single file with as many individual memory-mapped files as there are the columns in the original data source.

Because a Tableau data extract file is a memory-mapped file, when Tableau requests data from a .tde file, the data is loaded directly into the memory by the operating system. Tableau does not have to open, process, or decompress the file. If needed, the operating system continues to move data in and out of RAM to ensure that all of the requested data is made available to Tableau. It means that Tableau can query data that is bigger than the RAM on the computer.

For example, in the superstore dataset, you want to calculate the sum of profit for each product category. In the traditional data table, you have to go through each row to get the value of profit, and then sum them up for each product category. In TDE files, only columns **Product Category** and **Profit** are loaded into the memory. You can get the profit value straight line from one column.

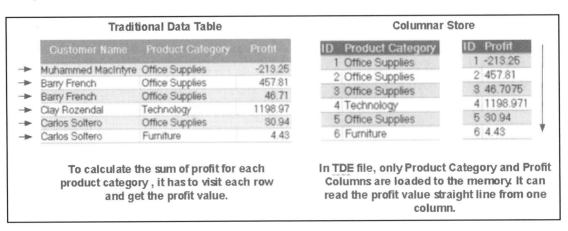

Traditional Data Table		
Customer Name	Product Category	Profit
Muhammed MacIntyre	Office Supplies	-213.25
Barry French	Office Supplies	457.81
Barry French	Office Supplies	46.71
Clay Rozendal	Technology	1198.97
Carlos Soltero	Office Supplies	30.94
Carlos Soltero	Furniture	4.43

Columnar Store			
ID	Product Category	ID	Profit
1	Office Supplies	1	-213.25
2	Office Supplies	2	457.81
3	Office Supplies	3	46.7075
4	Technology	4	1198.971
5	Office Supplies	5	30.94
6	Furniture	6	4.43

To calculate the sum of profit for each product category, it has to visit each row and get the profit value.

In TDE file, only Product Category and Profit Columns are loaded to the memory. It can read the profit value straight line from one column.

Benefits of using Tableau data extracts

The following are the seven main benefits of using Tableau data extract:

- **Enhanced performance**: Using Tableau data extracts can increase performance when the underlying data source is slow. It can also speed up CustomSQL.
- **Reduced load**: Using Tableau data extracts instead of a live connection to databases reduces the load on the database that can result from heavy traffic.
- **Portability**: Tableau data extracts can be bundled with the visualizations in a packaged workbook for sharing with others.
- **Pre-aggregation**: When creating extract, you can choose to aggregate your data for certain dimensions. An aggregated extract has a smaller size and contains only aggregated data. Accessing the values of aggregations in visualization is very fast since all of the work to derive the values has been done. You can choose the level of aggregation. For example, you can choose to aggregate your measures to month, quarter, or year.
- **Materialize calculated fields**: When you choose to optimize the extract, all of the calculated fields that have been defined are converted to static values upon the next full refresh. They become additional data fields, which can be accessed and aggregated as quickly as any other field in the extract. The improvement in performance can be significant, especially on string calculations, since string calculations are much slower compared to numeric or date calculations.
- **Publish to Tableau Public and Tableau Online**: Tableau Public only supports Tableau extract files. Though Tableau Online can connect to some cloud based data sources, Tableau data extract is the most commonly used.
- **Support for certain function not available when using live connection**: Certain functions, such as count distinct, are only available when using Tableau data extract.

Creating extract with large volume of data efficiently

In the previous section, we walked through the design principle of Tableau data extract and the benefit of using data extract. I believe you cannot wait to get your hands dirty and create some extracts by yourself. But you may run into the situation that it takes a very long time to create a data extract with a large volume of data. Luckily, we have some tips and tricks to make this process more efficient.

Loading a very large Excel file to Tableau

If you have an Excel file with lots of data and formulas, it could take a long time to load into Tableau. The best practice is to save the Excel file as a `.csv` file and remove all the formulas.

Aggregating the values to higher dimension

If you do not need the values down to the dimension of what it is in the underlying data source, aggregating to a higher dimension will significantly reduce the extract size and improve performance.

For example, in your data set, you have a date dimension, which has the value for each day. But you care only about the monthly values. To reduce the size of the extract while still meeting your analytics needs, you can aggregate the measures to month level.

The steps are as follows:

1. Right-click on the data you want to extract, and click on **Extract Data...**:

2. In the extract data window, you can check the **Aggregate data for visible dimensions** checkbox and select **Roll up dates to Month**:

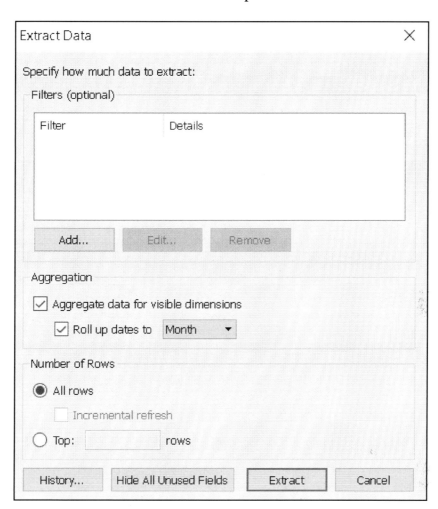

Using data source filter

Add a data source filter by right-clicking on the data source and then choosing **Edit Data Source Filter** to remove the data you do not need before creating the extract.

Hiding unused fields

Hiding unused fields before creating a data extract can speed up the process of extract creation and also save storage space.

Uploading and managing Tableau data extract in Tableau online

In the previous section, we learned about how to make the process of creating large data extract more efficient. After you create many data extracts, you may want to store and manage them in a centralized repository so they can be easily managed, updated, and shared with others. Tableau online is a good place for storing and managing data extracts. Now let's learn about how to upload and manage data extracts in Tableau online.

Creating workbook just for extracts

One way to create extracts is to create them in different workbooks. The advantage is that you can create extracts on the fly when you need them. But the disadvantage is that once you create many extracts, it is very difficult to manage them. You can hardly remember which dashboard has which extracts. A better solution is to create data extracts only in a workbook and then uploading the extracts to Tableau online. When you need to create visualizations, you can use the extracts in Tableau online. If you want to manage the extracts further, you can use different workbooks for different types of data sources. For example, you can use one workbook for Excel files, one workbook for local databases, one workbook for Web based data and so on.

Using default project

Store your data extracts in the default project. You cannot delete the default project, so you will not delete your data extracts accidentally. If you use a command line to refresh the data extracts, the project name is not needed if they are in the default project.

Making sure Tableau online/server has enough space

In Tableau Online/Server, it is important to allocate enough disk space to create new data extracts and store/refresh existing Tableau data extracts. At least two or three times the size of the data extracts is needed.

Refreshing Tableau data extracts

In the previous section, we learned about how to upload and manage data extracts in Tableau online. Once you have data extracts available to use for analytics, you also need to make sure that they are updated on a regular basis so you have the most up-to-date data for analytics. Tableau offers different ways of refreshing data extracts. Let's walk through each of them.

Refreshing published extracts locally

Here are some steps to refresh published extracts locally:

1. Log in to Tableau online, and click on the **Data Sources** tab:

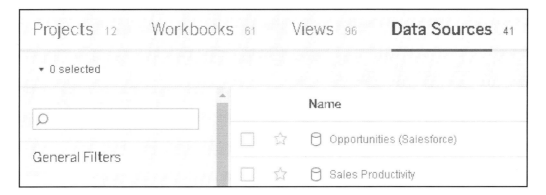

2. Look for the data extract that you want to refresh:

3. Download the data extract:

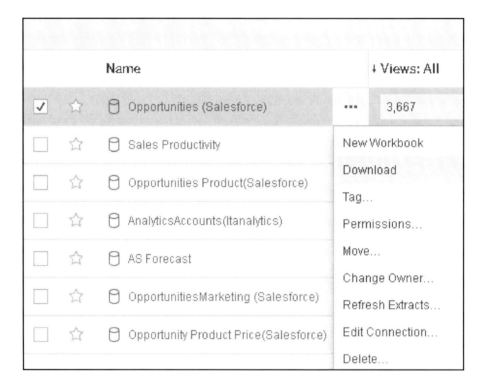

4. Open the data extract in Tableau desktop by double-clicking on the extract file. After opening the data extract file, right-click on data extract name, and click on **Extract | Refresh (Full)**:

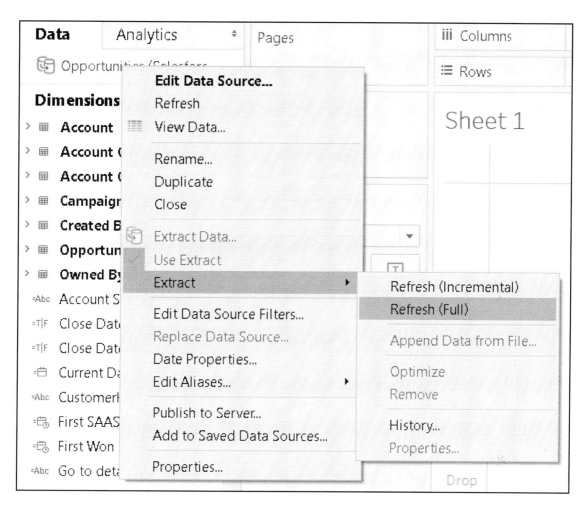

5. Once the refresh is done, right-click on the **data extract**, and click on **Publish to Server...**:

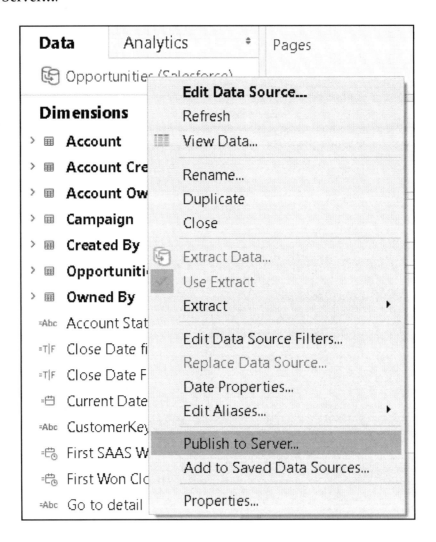

6. Click on **Yes** when you are asked if you want to overwrite the existing data extract:

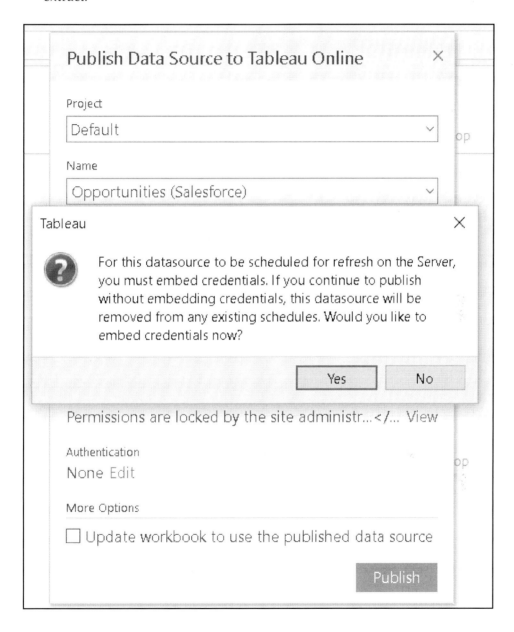

Schedule data extract refresh in Tableau Online

Cloud data sources (for example, Salesforce) can be refreshed using schedule jobs in Tableau online. One option is to use the Tableau Desktop command line to refresh data sources that are not in the cloud. Windows Scheduler can be used to automate the refresh jobs to update extracts via the Tableau Desktop command. Another option is to use the sync application or manually refresh the extracts using Tableau Desktop.

 Data extract name cannot include + when using command line to refresh the extract.

Incremental refresh

- Only new records from the underlying data source are added in incremental refresh. So the amount of time required to refresh the data extract is less. The incremental extract processes run even if there are no new records to add.
- Over time, incremental refresh performance gets worse. Incremental extracts only add new records, so the amount of data and the size of memory needed are growing.
- You cannot do incremental refreshes if you append another file to the data source.

Using Tableau web connector to create data extract

In the previous section, we learned about how to refresh data extract in different ways. With Tableau 10, you can use the Tableau web connector to connect to many web based data sources and create data extract.

What is Tableau web connector?

The **Tableau Web Data Connector** is the API that can be used by people who want to write some code to connect to certain web based data, such as a Web page.

The connectors can be written in Java. It seems that these web connectors can only connect to Web pages, Web services and so on. It can also connect to local files.

How to use Tableau web connector?

Click on **Data** | **New Data source** | **Web Data Connector**.

Is the Tableau web connection live?

The data is pulled when the connection is built, and Tableau will store the data locally in the Tableau extract. You can still refresh the data manually or via schedule jobs.

Are there any Tableau web connection available?

Here is a list of web connectors around the Tableau community:

- **Alteryx**: `http://data.theinformationlab.co.uk/alteryx.html`.
- **Facebook**: `http://tableaujunkie.com/post/123558558693/facebook-web-dat a-connector`.

You can check the tableau community for more web connectors.

Summary

Let's summarize the best practices for data extracts.

You should use full fresh instead of incremental refresh when it is possible. If you need to do incremental refresh, do a full refresh on those extracts on a regular basis. You can publish data extracts to Tableau Online/Server to avoid duplicates. You should hide unused fields or use filter before creating extracts to improve performance and save storage space. You need to have enough disk space for large extracts. A good way is to use SSD drivers.

In the next chapter, we will talk about how to combine different data together using data blending.

2
Data Blending

In the previous chapter, we talked about how to extract data from different data sources using Tableau data extract and keep them up to date. After connecting to different data sources, we want to combine them together in Tableau for data analytics. In this chapter, we will talk about how to combine different data sources together using data blending.

In this chapter, we will cover the following:

- Primary versus secondary data source in data blending
- Data blending versus join
- Potential issues of using data blending and quick fix
- Use cases of solving different business problems by blending the same data in different ways
- Domain padding
- Use Alteryx to blend a large volume of data efficiently

Primary versus secondary data source in data blending

The concept of primary and secondary data sources is very basic but very important. You cannot perform data blending without understanding this concept. Now let's learn about it, starting with the following points:

- When you decide which data source to use as the primary data source, you need to drag the dimension/measure to the view from that data source first.
- All secondary measures are aggregated.

- For each primary dimension, it can only map to one value in the secondary dimension. If the secondary dimension has one multiple values map to the primary dimension, it will show the values as *.

- Primary and secondary data sources can be blended on multiple fields, and the fields do not need to be in the visualizations.

- You can think of primary data source as left join secondary data source. However, the difference, as mentioned before, is that all secondary measures are aggregated, and for each primary dimension, it can only map to one value in the secondary dimension. If the secondary dimension has one multiple values map to the primary dimension, it will show the values as *. But the benefit of data blending over left join is that since blending is done before the aggregation, it will not introduce a duplicate. There is a more detailed example in the following section.

- Data blending is sheet specific. This means that you can have one data source as the primary data source in one sheet but as a secondary data source in another sheet.

- If there is no common key between the primary and secondary data sources, you can still blend them by grouping the key in another secondary data source into the secondary that does not have a common key with the primary. You need to create a help sheet, the primary data source is the no-common key secondary, then blend data on the key group. For example, in the superstore sample data provided by Tableau (you can search superstore Tableau and download the sample data), I want to analyze the sales for each vertical. But the vertical data is not available in the **Orders** table. It is in another Excel file that has the **Manager** name and the **Vertical** they own. Have a look at the following figure:

	A	B
1	Manager	Vertical
2	Chris	Telecom
3	Erin	Finance
4	Pat	Tech
5	Sam	Retail
6	William	Media

- In order to analyze the sales for each **Vertical**, I need to create a common key between the **Orders** table and the **Vertical** table. Although the **Vertical** table does not have a common key with the **Orders** table, it has a common key with the **Users** table in the superstore data set. The solution is to create a primary group to add the **Region** to the **Vertical** table as a join key. The following are the steps in detail:

   1. Connect to the data source that does not have a common key with the primary table. In this example, it is the **Vertical** table, and it does not have a common key with the **Orders** table.
   2. From the **Vertical** table, drag the **Manager** to the view. Since it is the first field in the view, the **Product** table becomes the primary data source in this **Help** sheet.
   3. Connect to the secondary data source that has the common key with the primary table. In this example, it is the **Users** table in the superstore data source, and it has a common key with the **Orders** table, which is **Region**.
   4. From the **Users** table, drag the **Region** to the view. The view shows the **Region** from the secondary data source (users) and all the managers associated with those regions. You will see that manager **Pat** has a region as *; this is because **Pat** is in multiple regions (**Central**, **East**,and **South**). This is shown in the following screenshot:

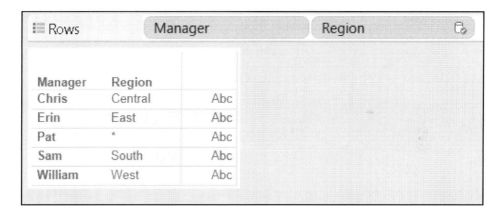

5. Right-click on the **Region** field and select **Create Primary Group**.

6. Pat does not belong to any group because he has multiple regions, so we just add him to the **Central** group:

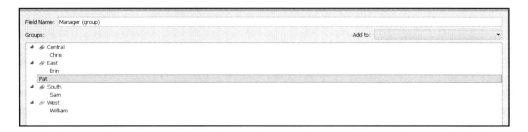

7. Choose the **Central** group in the **Add to** drop down list:

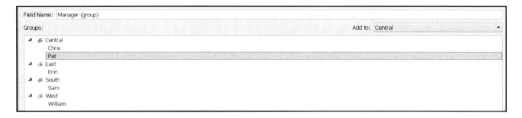

8. Click on **OK**. There is a new group in the **Vertical** table called **Manager (group)**. Since you have grouped the **Region** field into the **Vertical** table, you can now use it to blend with the **Orders** table.

9. From the **Orders** table, drag **Region** into the view. Since it is the first field in the view, the **Orders** table is the primary data source.

10. Click on **Data | Edit Relationships** to set the **Orders** table and the **Vertical** tables to be blended on **Region** and **Manager (group)**:

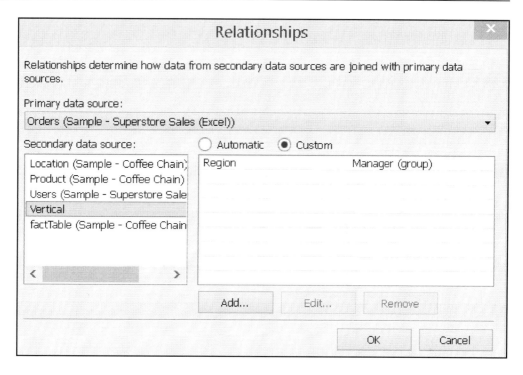

11. From **Vertical** table, drag the **Vertical** into the view.
12. From the **Orders** table, drag **Sales** into the view. Now you can see the **Sales** values for each **Vertical**. Since only the **West** region is mapped to the **Region** field in **Vertical**, we only see Sales for the west region:

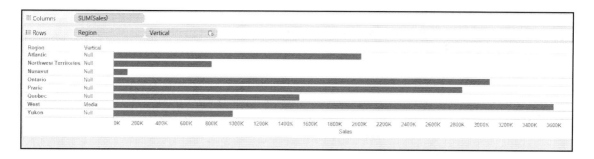

 The primary group is static, not dynamic. If you add new values to the Region field or the Manager field, you need to recreate the primary group.

Data blending versus join

In the previous section, we learned about the important concept of primary and secondary data sources. After understanding this concept, we can start blending data using the process of data blending. But you may wonder that both data blending and join and combine data together, when should I use which and why? Now let's answer these questions.

When to use data blending instead of joining

Joining can improve performance if the two connections in the workbook are from the same data source. Joining is also better when you try to add data to an existing data source in the same data connection. However, sometimes joining may not work as well as data blending. Common scenarios in which you should choose data blending instead of joining are as follows:

- There are many records in the data connections, and join is not possible.
- If you have multiple data connections, which are large and take a long time to query, using a join can significantly increase the query time. A better way is to aggregate the tables to a higher level and then blend the data on the aggregated fields. For example, you can aggregate data on the year rather than the exact date, or on the country instead of the city.
- You want to display a summary and the details at the same time.
- If you want to see both the summary of a calculation and the breakdown in the same view, select the data source from the Data menu, and then duplicate it. Then you can do a self-blending of the two same data sources. You can get the detail breakdown from the primary data source and the summary from the secondary data source (remember that all secondary measures are aggregated). You can also achieve the same goal using level of detail calculation, which is available in Tableau 9.0.
- Sometimes the numeric numbers coming from a data source that is joining multiple tables are not accurate. This is because join may introduce duplicates.
- For example, assume that you have the following two tables about airline tickets. Table one has **City ID**, **Departure City**, and **Number of Tickets Left**. Table two has the **City ID**, the **Website** that the tickets are sold, and **Number of Tickets sold**. The following table has the data of **City ID**, **Departure City**, and **Number of Tickets Left**:

City ID	Departure City	Number of Tickets Left
1A	NYC	11
2B	SF	22
3C	LA	33

- Another table, as shown next, has the data of **City ID**, **Website** to purchase air tickets, and **Number of Tickets Sold**:

City ID	Website	Number of Tickets Sold
1A	Expedia	5
2B	Expedia	3
3C	Expedia	6
1A	Priceline	2
2B	Priceline	7
3C	Priceline	3
1A	Kayak	5
2B	Kayak	1
3C	Kayak	6

- If you do an inner join of the two tables on **City ID**, the result is the following table. You will see that **Number of Tickets Left** for each **Departure City** is duplicated:

City ID	City ID (Sheet2)	Departure City	Website	Number of Records	Number of Tickets Left	Number of Tickets Sold
1A	1A	NYC	Expedia	1	11	5
1A	1A	NYC	Kayak	1	11	5
1A	1A	NYC	Priceline	1	11	2
2B	2B	SF	Expedia	1	22	3
2B	2B	SF	Kayak	1	22	1
2B	2B	SF	Priceline	1	22	7
3C	3C	LA	Expedia	1	33	6
3C	3C	LA	Kayak	1	33	6
3C	3C	LA	Priceline	1	33	3

- If you drag the **Departure City** and **Number of Tickets Left** fields to the view, the view shows that **Number of Tickets Left** for **LA** is **99** instead of 33:

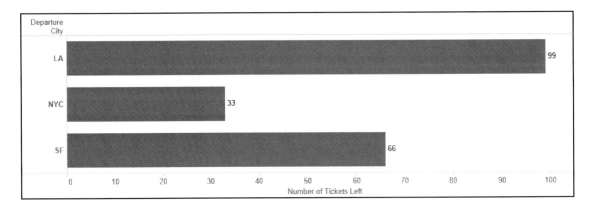

If you use data blending instead of join, you will not have this duplicate issue.

Differences between data blending and join

The following table is a great summary of differences between data blending and left join. Thanks to Jonathan Drummey for sharing this in his presentation *Think Data Thursday: Data Blending – How it is like and not like a Left Join*, as shown next:

	Left Join	Data Blend
Source	All tables in one source	Anything you want
Control	Fixed in the data source	Per worksheet – blend can change based on dragging and dropping pills
Granularity	Record level	Post aggregation (after record-level, LOD calcs, and regular aggregates are computed)
What can link	Exact values	Dimensions after record-level calcs, LOD calcs, and densification
Limits in using fields	None	Have to be aware of granularity of data, blend, and view – secondary dims can't increase granularity, non-additive aggregates (COUNTD() are limited, etc.
Performance	As fast as your data source	Adds overhead, limited to 100s of thousands distinct linking values

Potential issues of using data blending and quick fix

In the previous section, we talked about when to use data blending and when to use join and the differences between them. Although data blending has lots of benefits, you may run into some issues when using this process. Now let's walk through some common issues stumbled upon when using data blending and the quick fix for these issues.

Blend on date

Sometimes you may see weird results or * if you perform blending on a date field. Make sure you are blending not only the date field but also `Day (Date)`, `Week (Date)`, `Month (Date)`, `Quarter (Date)`, `Year (Date)` or any other type of aggregated date fields.

Use table calculations to aggregate blended data

Sometimes you may want to blend two data sources at a deeper level of detail but show an aggregated value at a higher level in the view. There are three options to do this:

- Do not use data blending. Use join or Custom SQL or a query outside of Tableau. But if you are trying to do this for different types of data sources, for example, Salesforce and MySQL, it could be difficult.
- Use the primary group feature, which has been mentioned before, to group the details from the secondary data source into the primary data source. The drawback is that the group is not dynamic. You have to create the group again to incorporate any changes on either field in the group
- Perform blending on the deeper level of detail, then use table calculations to do the aggregation.
- For example, in the Coffee Chain sample data source, I want to see what the total number of decaf products is and what the profit of each decaf product is in the same view. To show the profit by product, I need to have the **Product ID** in the view, but to show the total number of decaf products, I do not want the product id in the view. In order to achieve my goal, I will perform the following steps:
  1. I first blend **factTable** tale in the Coffee Chain data source with **Product** table on **Product ID**.
  2. Drag the **Product ID** from **factTable** to the color shelf in view so **factTable** is the primary data source.
  3. Drag **Type** from the secondary to the view as the **filter**. Choose include **Decaf only**.
  4. In the **Product data** source, create a calculation called `Decaf Products`:

  5. In the **Product** data source, create another calculation called `Total Decaf Products`:

```
Total Decaf Products                    Product (Sample - Coffee Chain)

Results are computed along Table (Across).  Totals summarize values from Table (Across).
IF FIRST()==0 THEN
    TOTAL([Decaf Products])
END
```

6. Drag `Total Decaf Products` to the view. Set the **Compute using** as **Product ID**.

7. Drag the **Profit** in the **factTable** to the view. You will see that **Total Decaf Products** is not broken down by **Product ID** but **Profit** is:

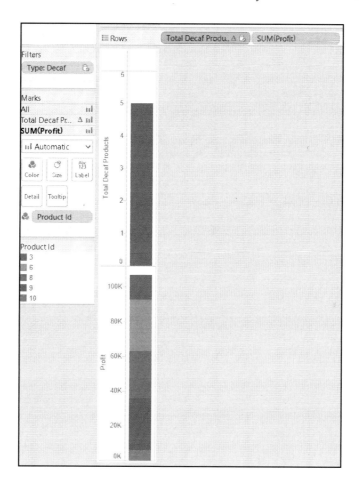

Use cases of solving different business problems by blending the same data in different ways

In the previous section, we talked about some common issues when using data blending and some quick fix. When using data blending to analyze data and solve real business questions, you may be surprised that you can solve completely different business questions by blending the same data in different ways. Now let's look at some examples.

Performing Blend on single field versus multiple fields

A great thing about data blending is that by blending different fields of the same data sources, you can solve different business problems. Now let's look at an example of blending a single field vs blending multiple fields.

For example, you have one table that has the sales data for customers; have a look at the following screenshot:

Customer Name	Product Name	Sales	Website
MJ	Crab	10	Fresh
Ken	Fish	20	Fresh
Go	Crab	20	Delivery
MJ	Shrimp	20	Delivery
Go	Fish	30	Fresh

You have another table that has the **Coupons** received by customers, as shown in the following screenshot:

Customer Name	Product	Coupon	Channel
MJ	Fish	1	email
MJ	Shrimp	1	app
Go	Shrimp	1	app
Go	Crab	1	email
Ken	Fish	1	email

Now let's look at the scenario of performing blending on a single field. The business question I want to answer is: what is the total sale for each customer and how many coupons have they received? To answer this question, I will build the following Viz:

1. Drag **Customer Name** from **Sales** table to **Rows**.
2. Drag **Sales** from **Sales** table to **Columns**.
3. Drag **Coupon** from **Coupon** table to **Columns**.
4. Set the **blending key** as **Customer Name**. You will see the following visualization in the view:

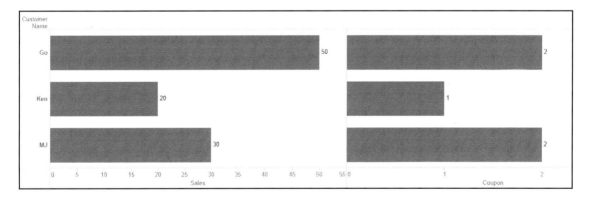

Now let's look at the scenario of blending multiple fields. The business question I want to answer is: how many coupons did each customer use and what is the sales for using those coupons? To answer this question, I will build the following Viz:

1. Drag **Customer Name** from **Sales** table to **Rows**.
2. Drag **Sales** from **Sales** table to **Columns**.
3. Drag **Coupon** from **Coupon** table to **Columns**.

4. Set the **blending key** as **Customer Name** and **Product/Product Name**.

5. Drag **Product** from **Coupon** table to the view as a filter, set the filter as **Exclude Null**. You will see the following Viz in the view:

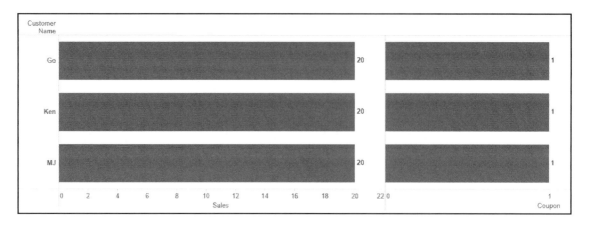

Since you are performing blending on both **Customer Name** and **Product** and bringing in the **Filter** to keep the products that exist in both primary and secondary data source, it will show the product that is purchased by using coupons. In the previous scenario, since we are not performing blending on product, we will see the total sales for all the products that each customer purchased and the total number of coupons they received, not necessarily how many they used.

With data blending, we are able to answer two different business questions with the same data sets just by blending different data fields.

Self-blending

Self-Blending is a great way to solve some complex problems. One common business question asked is how to show my sales of the current and previous years in the same view. You can create the following Viz to answer his question:

1. Drag the **Order Date** from the **Orders** table from the Superstore data set onto **Columns**. Set it at **year** level.
2. Drag the **Sales** from the **Orders** table from the Superstore data set onto **Rows**.
3. Duplicate the **Orders** table from the Superstore data set.

4. Create a calculation in the duplicated data set called `Order Date Year`:

5. Set the **Orders** table and the duplicated **Orders** table to perform blend on **Year(Order Date)** and **Order Date year**.
6. Rename the **Sales** in the duplicated Orders table as **Sales Last Year**.
7. Drag **Sales Last Year** to **Rows**.
8. Drag the **Measure names** onto the Color shelf. You will see the following Viz:

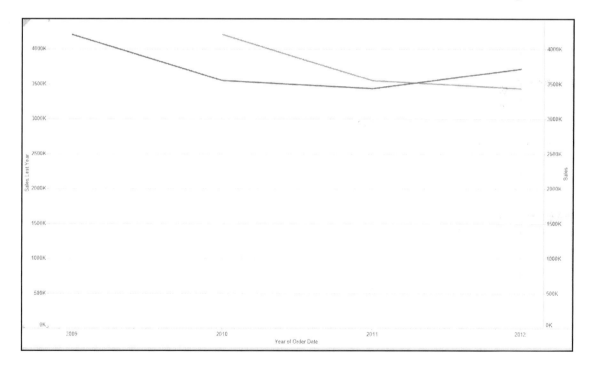

In the Viz, you can see that by shifting the **Order Date Year** from the duplicated secondary data source, we are able to show the sales from the current and previous years in the same Viz.

Domain padding

Domain padding is not a common use case with blending. You may have the data blending field in the secondary data sources, but some values in the blending key of the secondary data source are missing from the primary data source. You may also have values in the primary blending key that are missing from the secondary data source. For example, if your blending key is **date**, there might be some extract dates in the secondary data source but not in the primary data source. You may also have some dates in the primary data sources that are missing from the secondary data source.

To solve this issue, you have three options.

- The first one is to add the missing values to the primary data source.
- The second is to use Custom SQL.
- The third is to use the **Show Missing Values** feature in Tableau.

For example, you have a primary data source that has a Date field and a Value field. Take a look at the following screenshot:

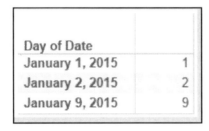

Your secondary data source also has a Date field and a Value field, as shown in the following screenshot:

Day of Date	
January 1, 2015	1
January 2, 2015	2
January 6, 2015	6
January 7, 2015	7

If you just blend the two data sources without turning on **Show Missing Values**, you will only see values for **January 1** and **January 2** since January 6 and January 7 are missing from the primary data source:

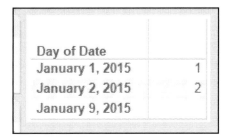

If you turn on the **Show Missing Values** option, you will see values for **January 6** and **January 7**:

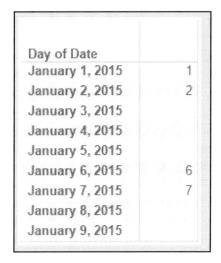

 The **Show Missing Values** feature only works for Date & Time or Date data type or Bins. It also does not work for Exact Date for a Date&Time data type field. But it works for Exact Date for a Date data type field.

Using Alteryx to blend large volume of data efficiently

Tableau's data blending feature is great. But it suffers from bad performance when blending very large datasets. Alteryx is a tool that has displayed a great performance when blending large data and also integrates with Tableau.

Getting started with Alteryx

Alteryx is used for data blending, data preparation, and advanced data analytics, such as predictive analytics. Alteryx is very easy to use, so the business users can perform advanced analytics.

Benefit of Alteryx

Alteryx is very good for blending large volumes of data and then feeding into Tableau. Alteryx can also perform full outer join, which Tableau does not. Alteryx can export the blended data as `.tde` file or publish directly to Tableau server/online.

To learn more about Alteryx, visit their website at `http://www.alteryx.com/`.

Summary

In summary, you should keep in mind the following best practices for data blending: you should choose Data Blending or Join based on your use case. You should always choose the data source with the lowest level of detail coming from as the primary data source since all measures from secondary source are aggregated. You can set up the blending key differently based on your use case to solve different business questions. You should remember to use self-blending. You can use domain padding to show missing values on Date.

In the next chapter, we will learn about the advanced use cases of calculations and parameters.

3

Calculation/Parameter

In the previous chapter, we talked about how to blend data from different data sources using data blending. After blending different data sources together, we want to create calculations for data analytics. In this chapter, we will talk about the advanced use cases of calculations and parameters.

In this chapter, we will cover the following:

- Table calculations
- LOD calculations
- Date calculations
- String calculations
- Count
- Custom total
- Dynamic parameter

Table calculations

It is critical to master the use of table calculations to become a Tableau master. Now let's go deep into every aspect you need to know about table calculations.

Overview

Table calculations are calculations that are computed using the values in the entire table in the view. For example, the running total in the quick table calculation is computed using all the values in the column of the selected measure.

There are many ways to create table calculations in Tableau:

- You can create your own calculation using the table calculation functions.
- You can also click on the measure, and choose Quick Table Calculation.
- You can click on the measure, and choose Add Table Calculation, and then choose Edit Table Calculation to get the results you need.

Key concepts

Table calculation is very useful and easy to use. But when you try to apply it to complex data analytics, you may feel that the results of the table calculation is not what you expect. To master table calculations, you need to have a very good understanding of addressing and partitioning.

Understand addressing and partitioning

The most important thing in table calculations is to set the Compute Using. When we are setting the compute using, we are setting the addressing. The addresses, which are also called rows in the partition, are distinct combinations of values of the dimensions used for addressing. Tableau computes one table calculation result for each address.

Let's look at an example of the `INDEX()` function using the **Orders** table from the Superstore data source. The Index calculation is a simple function of `INDEX()`:

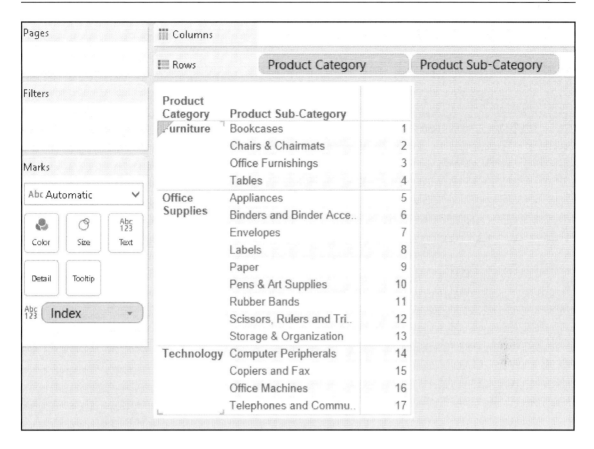

The addressing is **Compute Using Table (Down)**. In this example, it means that the addressing is on **Product Category** and **Product Sub-Category**. Tableau is computing the table calculation result for each combination of the **Product Category** and **Product Sub-Category**.

All of the dimensions in the view that are not part of the addressing are automatically becoming part of the partitioning. Tableau will restart calculating the table calculation for each new distinct combination of the values of the dimensions in partitioning. The definition of restart is dependent on the particular table calculation function. In the case of INDEX(), restart means starting back at one. So if we set the Compute Using (addressing) of the INDEX() to **Product Sub-Category**, it will partition (restart) on each Product Category, as shown in the following screenshot:

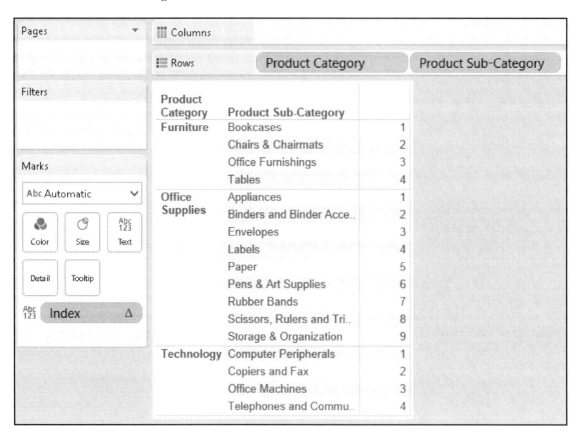

As the dimensions are added to the view, they are automatically becoming part of the partitioning. For example, in the Orders table of the Superstore data source, we have the % of Total Profit table calculation, that is Compute Using (addressing) on Order Date, as shown next:

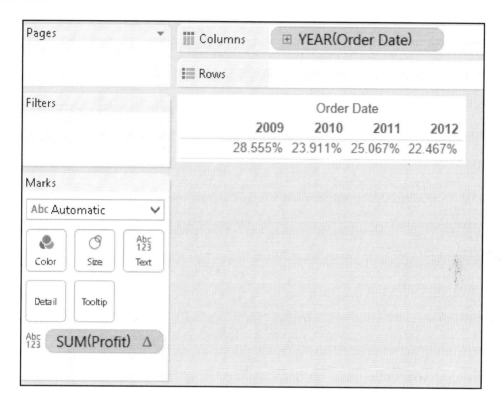

And then we add the `Product Category` to the view, Tableau will automatically add Product Category to partition and continue to Compute Using (addressing) Order Date:

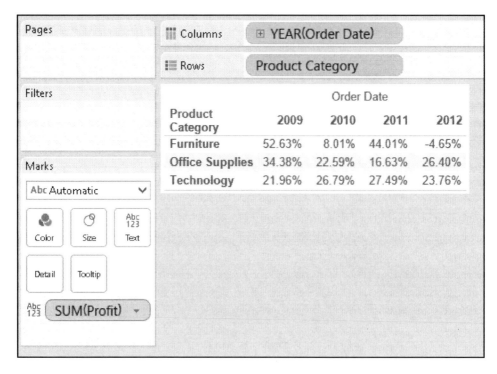

If I expand the Order Date from Year to Quarter, you will see the % of Total is Compute Using `Quarter (Order Date)` and partition on **Product Category**:

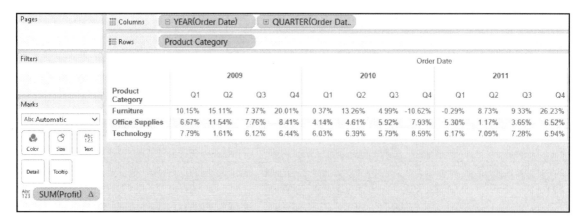

If I want to have a table calculation result for each Year & Product Category, what should I Compute Using? First, let's think about partitions, which are the boundaries of table calculations. Currently there are three dimensions in the View: Year, Quarter, and Product Category. If I want to partition on Year and Product Category, I need to Compute Using (addressing) Quarter. However, Quarter is not part of the Compute Using option. We can use the Edit Table Calculation option to set up the addressing we want. In the "Summarize the values from" dropdown list, choose the Advanced option, and it will open the advanced dialog box:

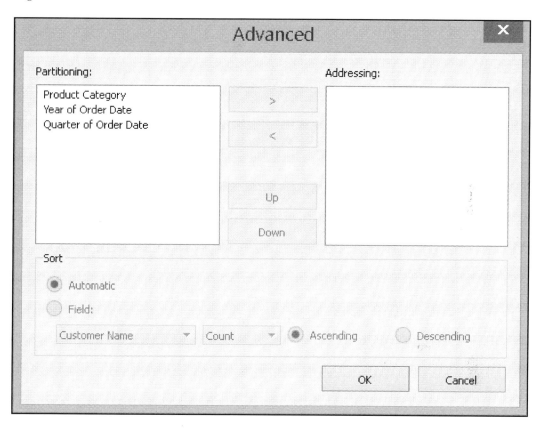

It shows all the dimensions in the view. On the left side, you will see all the dimensions that are part of the partitioning. On the right side, you will see all the dimensions that are part of the addressing. The order of the dimensions for addressing is very important because it determines how those dimensions are going to be sorted for the table calculations, and it also affects At the Level, which we will discuss in the next section.

We can see that Tableau now includes both `Year of Order Date` and `Quarter of Order Date` as dimensions. I can choose Quarter of Order Date to be the addressing:

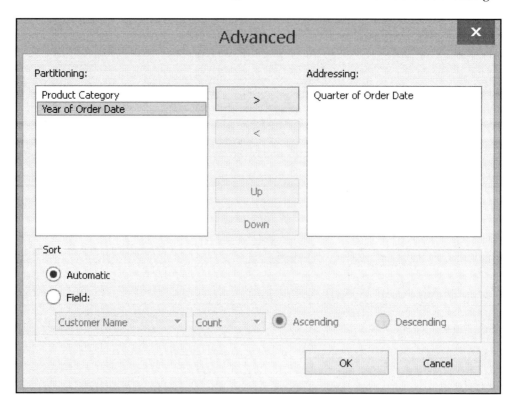

Now you can see that my table calculation is partition on `Year (Order Date)` and `Product Category,` addressing on `Quarter (Order Date)`:

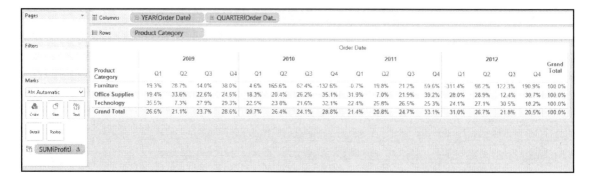

Understanding At the Level

At the Level is kind of confusing because it behaves differently for the three categories of table calculations:

- Ordinal calculations, such as INDEX(), FIRST(), LAST(), SIZE(), LOOKUP(), and RANK()

- WINDOW_, RUNNING_, and the R script are all aggregate measures along the addresses of each partition

- TOTAL() is an aggregation of the inner measure at a different level of detail. At the Level has no effect on TOTAL()

We will focus on the At the Level for ordinal calculations. If we set the Compute Using (addressing) of the INDEX() to Product Sub-Category, it will partition (restart) on each Product Category, as shown in the following screenshot:

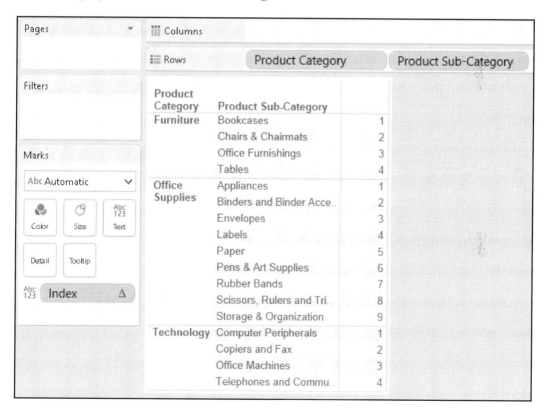

The At the level option is grayed out in the Edit table calculation box:

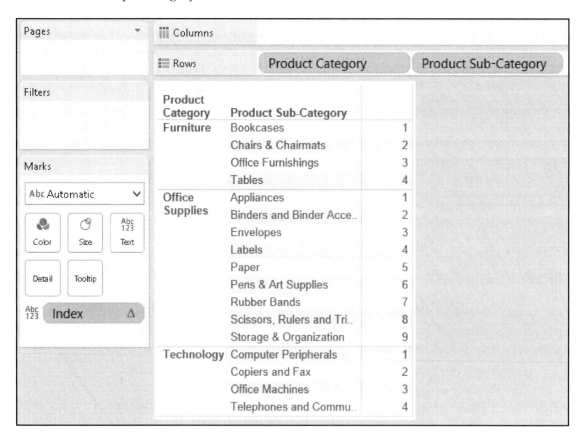

The reason that At the Level is grayed out is that it is only available when there are two or more addressing dimensions in the view. Currently, there is only one addressing dimension, which is Product Sub-Category.

If we select Compute Using as Advanced, and then we include both Product Category and Product Sub-Category into the addressing section of , we will see the At the Level is now available, as shown in the following screenshot:

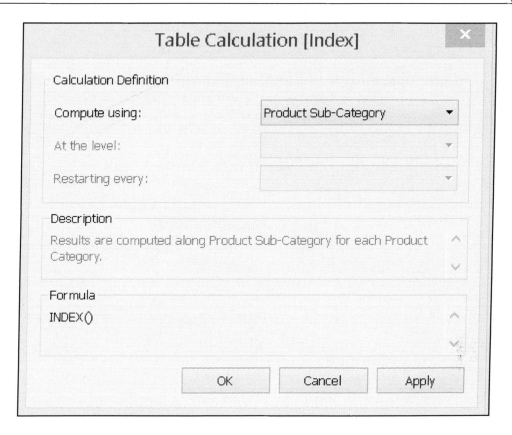

In the previous section, we talked about addressing and partitioning. The next concept we need to understand is At the Level.

Understanding At the Level options

When we click on the dropdown list of At the level, we see three options: Deepest, Product Category, and Product Sub-Category. Only the addressing dimensions and Deepest will show as the At the level options. If you choose Deepest, Tableau will set At the Level to be the dimension that is the last one in the dropdown list. If you specify a dimension other than Deepest for At the level, and then later add some other dimensions to the addressing section below the At the Level dimension you specified, Tableau will keep At the level as the dimension you specified. A good practice is to bring in all the dimensions you need and then specify the At the level dimension.

For the previous example, if we choose Deepest or the last dimension on the list. which is Product Sub-Category, there is no change in the result of the table calculation. If we choose a higher level dimension, which is Product Category, the addressing is on Product Category, Product Sub-Category, At the level Product Category, the result of the table calculation changes, as shown in the following screenshot:

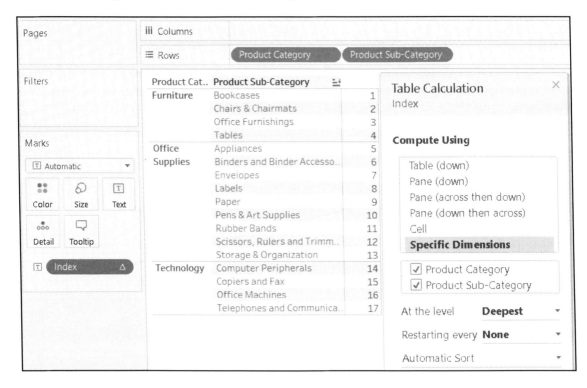

Since we are performing addressing on all the dimensions in the view, there is only one partition which is the entire view. Tableau will only increase the INDEX() table calculation value for each new Product Category, but it will return a value for every addressing in the partition. I'll walk through this table calculation process for the first several rows:

- Furniture/Bookcases is the first addressing and gets an Index of 1.

- Furniture/Chairs & Chairmats is the next addressing and has the same value as Product Category, so the Index is not increased and remains 1.

- Furniture/Office Furnishings still has the same value of Product Category, so the Index is still 1.

- Furniture/Tables still has the same value of Product Category, so the Index is still 1.

- Office/Supplies Appliances has a new value of Product Category, so the Index is increased to 2.

- Office Supplies/Binders and Binder Accessories has the same value of Product Category, so the Index is not incremented and remains 2.

And so on…

Tableau is following the same process for all of the ordinal calculations, as shown in the following screenshot:

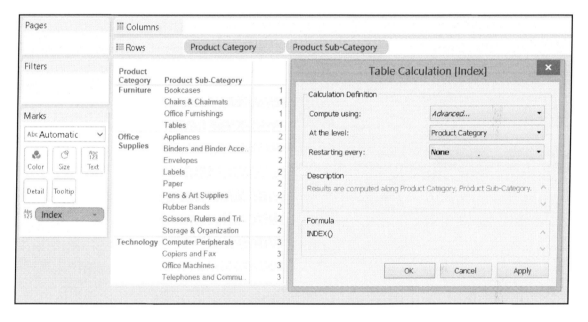

The SIZE() is only increasing in the Product Category column. Since there are Product Categories, every addressing gets a value of 3. The FIRST() is only increasing in the Product Category column. All the values of FIRST() for Furniture have the same value of 0 , which is the number of rows from the current Product Category to the first Product Category in the view. And all the values for Office Supplies have the same value of -1, all the values for Technology have the same value of -2 and so on. LAST() has the same logic as FIRST().

To summarize, for At the level addressing dimension and the all the addressing dimensions above the At the level addressing dimension, Tableau will increase the value of the ordinal table calculations. If you choose At the level as "Deepest" or the last dimension in the At the level dropdown list, Tableau will increase the value of the ordinal table calculations for each addressing dimension. If you choose a higher level addressing dimension, Tableau will increase the value of the ordinal table calculations for At the level addressing dimension.

One important thing to notice is that the rules above only apply to the addressing dimensions. If I add another dimension into the view, such as YEAR(Order Date), it is automatically added to the partitioning dimension so the table calculation will restart for each new Year(Order Date), as shown in the following screenshot:

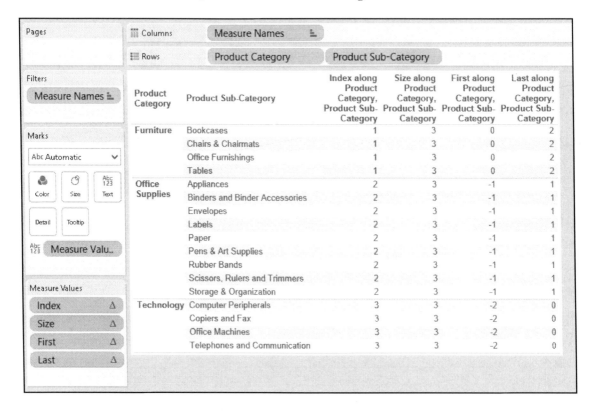

If you check the table calculation definition, you will see that YEAR(Order Date) is automatically added to the partitioning dimension:

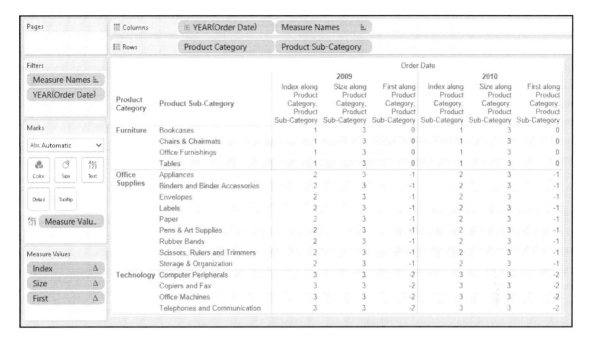

If we add `Year(Order Date)` to the first of the addressing dimensions and keep At the level as Product Category, we will get a different result, as shown in the following screenshot:

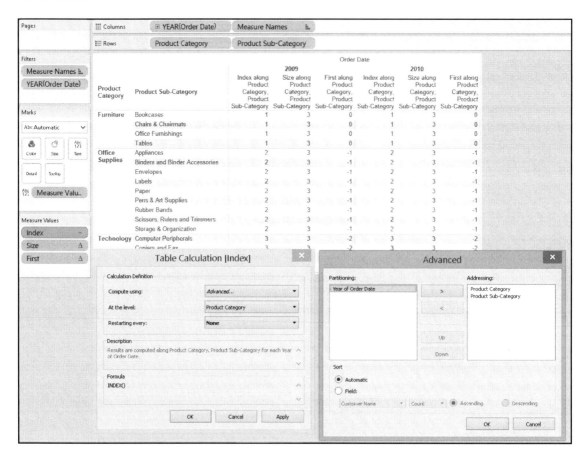

Based on rules discussed before, Tableau is increasing the table calculation for each new combination of Year(Order Date) and Product Category, but it will not increase the value for each Product Sub-Category within those dimensions.

Table calculation functions

Now let's look at some frequently used table calculation functions.

- FIRST (): This function is used to get the number of rows from the first row to the current row in the partition. For example, if the current row is the third row in the partition, FIRST () = −2.

- INDEX (): This function is used to get the index of the current row in the partition. The first row has an index of 1. For example, if the current row is the third row in the partition, INDEX () = 3.

- LAST (): This function is used to get the number of rows from the last row to the current row in the partition. For example, if the current row is the third row and there are 6 rows in the partition, LAST () = 3.

- LOOKUP (expression, [offset]): This function is used to get the value of the expression based on the value of the offset from the current row. For example, if the current row is the third row in the partition, LOOKUP (SUM([Sales]),2) is returning the SUM([Sales]) values in the fifth row.

- RUNNING_AVG(expression): This function is used to get the average of the values from the first row to the current row in the partition. For example, if the current row is the third row, RUNNING AVG(SUM([Sales]) is returning the average of SUM(Sales)) from the first row to the third row.

- RUNNING_COUNT(expression): This function is used to get the count of the values from the first row to the current row in the partition. For example, if the current row is the third row, RUNNING COUNT(SUM([Sales]) is returning the count of SUM(Sales)) from the first row to the third row.

- RUNNING_MAX(expression): This function is used to get the maximum of the values from the first row to the current row in the partition. For example, if the current row is the third row, RUNNING MAX(SUM([Sales]) is returning the maximum of SUM(Sales)) from the first row to the third row.

- RUNNING_MIN(expression): This function is used to get the minimum of the values from the first row to the current row in the partition. For example, if the current row is the third row, RUNNING MIN(SUM([Sales]) is returning the minimum of SUM(Sales)) from the first row to the third row.

- RUNNING_SUM(expression): This function is used to get the sum of the values from the first row to the current row in the partition. For example, if the current row is the third row, RUNNING SUM(SUM([Sales]) is returning the sum of SUM(Sales)) from the first row to the third row.

- SIZE (): This function is used to get the number of rows in the partition. For example, if there are 6 rows in the partition, SIZE () = 6.

- WINDOW_AVG(expression, [start, end]): This function is used to get the average in the defined window. The window is defined by the offset from the current row. For example, WINDOW_AVG(SUM([Sales]),FIRST (),and 0) is returning the average of SUM([Sales]) from the first row to the current row.
- WINDOW_COUNT(expression, [start, end]): This function is used to get the count in the defined window. The window is defined by the offset from the current row. For example, WINDOW_COUNT(SUM([Sales]),FIRST (),and 0) is returning the count of SUM([Sales]) from the first row to the current row.
- WINDOW_MAX(expression, [start, end]): This function is used to get the maximum in the defined window. The window is defined by the offset from the current row. For example, WINDOW_MAX(SUM([Sales]), FIRST (), 0) is returning the maximum of SUM([Sales]) from the first row to the current row.
- WINDOW_MIN(expression, [start, end]): This function is used to get the minimum in the defined window. The window is defined by the offset from the current row. For example, WINDOW_MIN(SUM([Sales]),FIRST (),and 0) is returning the minimum of SUM([Sales]) from the first row to the current row.
- WINDOW_SUM(expression, [start, end]): This function is used to get the sum in the defined window. The window is defined by the offset from the current row. For example, WINDOW_SUM(SUM([Sales]),FIRST (),and 0) is returning the sum of SUM([Sales]) from the first row to the current row.

Understand rank functions

Rank function can be very tricky to use sometimes. Tableau takes the following steps when calculating Rank function:

- Tableau will do the calculation starting with the partition that is composed of the At the level dimension and the addressing dimension that is above the At the level dimension in the At the level dropdown list. Let's call these partitions addressing partitions.

- For each aforementioned addressing partition, Tableau will use the unique combinations of values of dimension(s) that are below the At the level dimension as addresses, which are the rows in each addressing partition.

- The dimension sort of the view defines the position of the Rank function. The first position is the first address in each addressing partition, the second position is the second address and so on.

- The ranking positions are used to create the ranking partiitions, which is the slice of all addresses that are going to be ranked together. All of the addresses in the first ranking position create the first ranking partition, all of the addresses in the second position create the second ranking partition and so on.

- The addresses in each ranking partition are sorted by the measure in the Rank function, restarting every ranking partition.

- The rank is calculated to each address and restarted for each ranking partition.

Now let's look at some examples.

Example 1:

Let's create a simple data set as follows:

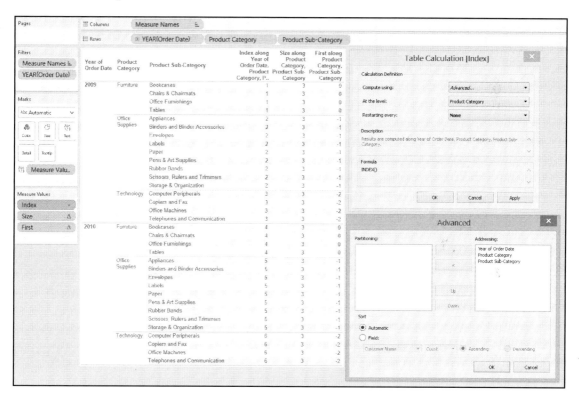

Now let's do a `RANK_UNIQUE(SUM[Sales]),'asc')`. Set the Compute Using on Group and Customer Name, and At the level Group. Since all the dimensions in the view are part of the addressing, the partition is the entire view, as shown in the following screenshot:

Group	Customer Name	Sales
1	A	60
2	B	60
2	C	60
3	D	80

Let me walk you through the steps of the calculation:

1. There are three addressing partitions based on Group 1, 2, and 3 since Group is the At the level dimension and no dimension is above it.
2. There are four addresses in the partition based on Customer Name since Customer Name is the dimension that is below the At the level dimension Group.
3. Here is how the ranking positions are calculated:

   - Group 1 Customer Name A is in addressing partition 1, position 1
   - Group 2 Customer Name B is in addressing partition 2, position 1
   - Group 2 Customer Name C is in addressing partition 2, position 2 (it is the second address in addressing partition 2)
   - Group 3 Customer Name D is in addressing partition 3, position 1

4. Now the ranking partitions are created based on the positions:

   - Group 1 Customer Name A is in ranking position 1
   - Group 2 Customer Name B is in ranking position 1
   - Group 2 Customer Name C is in ranking position 2
   - Group 3 Customer Name D is in ranking position 1

5. The ranking partitions are sorted by the measure (`SUM[Sales]`)) then alphanumerically for the dimensions that have the same value of the measure:
   - Ranking partition 1:
     - Value 60 Group 1 Customer Name A
     - Value 60 Group 2 Customer Name B
     - Value 80 Group 3 Customer Name D

- Ranking partition 2:
    - Value 60 Group 2 Customer Name C

6. The RANK_UNIQUE is applied:
    - Ranking partition 1:
        - Rank 1 Value 60 Group 1 Customer Name A
        - Rank 2 Value 60 Group 2 Customer Name B
        - Rank 3 Value 80 Group 3 Customer Name D
    - Ranking partition 2:
        - Rank 1 Value 60 Group 2 Customer Name C

When we see the view with Group and Customer Name as dimensions, the results of the RANK_UNIQUE may seem wield, but actually Tableau is following the aforementioned logic to calculate the results.

Example 2:

In this example, I am going to add a row for Group 2 Customer Name A with Sales of 60. It means that there are now 3 positions for Group 2, so there are 3 ranking partitions.

This is what the step 6 results will look like:

1. Ranking partition 1:

    - Rank 1 Value 60 Group 1 Customer Name A

    - Rank 2 Value 60 Group 2 Customer Name A

    - Rank 3 Value 80 Group 3 Customer Name D

2. Ranking partition 2:
    - Rank 1 Value 60 Group 2 Customer Name B
3. Ranking partition 3:
    - Rank 1 Value 60 Group 2 Customer Name C

Again, the result looks wield because the At the level is Group:

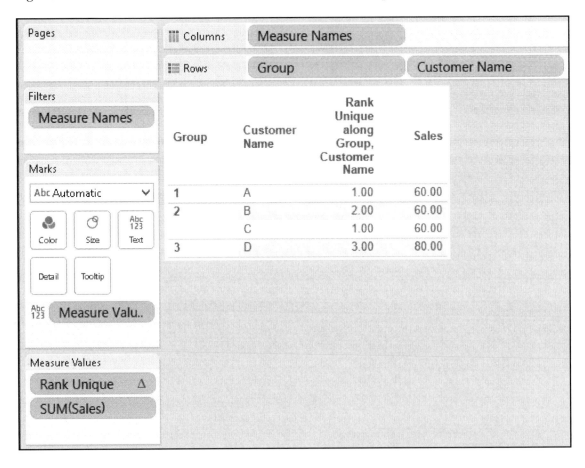

Example 3:

In this example, I am using the Superstore data set with Product Category & Product Containers as the dimensions where the table calculation will be
`RANK_UNIQUE(MIN([Product Category]),'asc')` with an Advanced Compute Using on Product Category & Product Container At the Level Product Category:

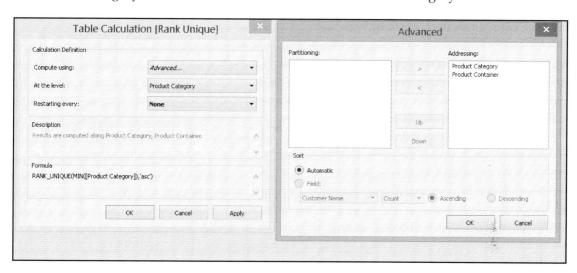

The result is as follows:

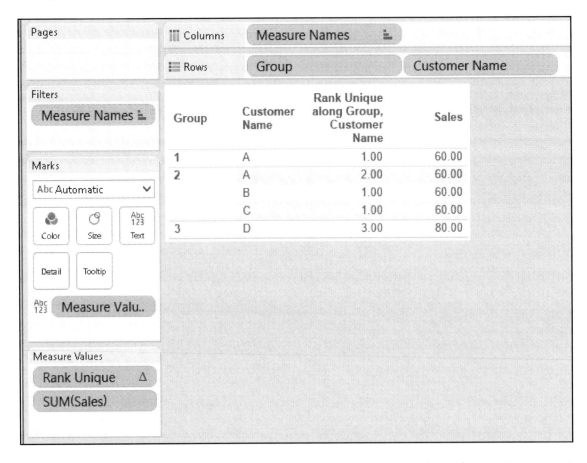

The reason why Technology/Wrap Bag gets a 2 is due to the same aforementioned process; I will walk through it:

1. There are three addressing partitions on Product Category: Furniture, Office Supplies, and Technology.
2. There are 20 addresses (7 for Furniture, 6 for Office Supplies, and 7 for Technology).

3. The addressing partition addresses with the ranking position number are as follows:

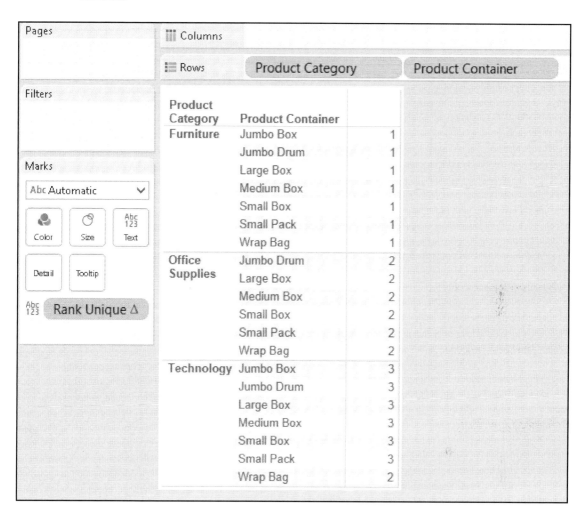

4. The ranking partitions are as follows:

Product Category	Product Container	
Furniture	Jumbo Box	1
	Jumbo Drum	2
	Large Box	3
	Medium Box	4
	Small Box	5
	Small Pack	6
	Wrap Bag	7
Office Supplies	Jumbo Drum	1
	Large Box	2
	Medium Box	3
	Small Box	4
	Small Pack	5
	Wrap Bag	6
Technology	Jumbo Box	1
	Jumbo Drum	2
	Large Box	3
	Medium Box	4
	Small Box	5
	Small Pack	6
	Wrap Bag	7

5. The ranking partitions are sorted by measure (MIN([Product Category])). It does not change anything from step 4.

6. The RANK_UNIQUE is applied in each ranking partition:

Rank Unique	Product Category	Product Container
1	Furniture	Jumbo Box
	Office Supplies	Jumbo Drum
	Technology	Jumbo Box
2	Furniture	Jumbo Drum
	Office Supplies	Large Box
	Technology	Jumbo Drum
3	Furniture	Large Box
	Office Supplies	Medium Box
	Technology	Large Box
4	Furniture	Medium Box
	Office Supplies	Small Box
	Technology	Medium Box
5	Furniture	Small Box
	Office Supplies	Small Pack
	Technology	Small Box
6	Furniture	Small Pack
	Office Supplies	Wrap Bag
	Technology	Small Pack
7	Furniture	Wrap Bag
	Technology	Wrap Bag

Example 4:

Now let's look at Rank on Dates. I am using the Order Date from the Superstore data set. I have added `YEAR(Order Date)` and `Quarter(Order Date)` as dimensions and filtered out 2009 Q3:

Rank Unique	Product Category	Product Container	
1	Furniture	Jumbo Box	1
	Office Supplies	Jumbo Drum	2
	Technology	Jumbo Box	3
2	Furniture	Jumbo Drum	1
	Office Supplies	Large Box	2
	Technology	Jumbo Drum	3
3	Furniture	Large Box	1
	Office Supplies	Medium Box	2
	Technology	Large Box	3
4	Furniture	Medium Box	1
	Office Supplies	Small Box	2
	Technology	Medium Box	3
5	Furniture	Small Box	1
	Office Supplies	Small Pack	2
	Technology	Small Box	3
6	Furniture	Small Pack	1
	Office Supplies	Wrap Bag	2
	Technology	Small Pack	3
7	Furniture	Wrap Bag	1
	Technology	Wrap Bag	2

I have added two Rank calculations. One is
`RANK_UNIQUE(DATEPART('quarter',MIN([Order Date])), 'asc')`, and the other is
`RANK_UNIQUE(DATETRUNC('quarter',MIN([Order Date])), 'asc')`; both have an
Advanced Compute Using on **Quarter of Order Date**, **Year of Order Date**, and **At the Level
Quarter of Order Date**. The result is as follows:

Year of Order Date	Quarter of Order Date	
2009	Q1	Abc
	Q2	Abc
	Q4	Abc
2010	Q1	Abc
	Q2	Abc
	Q3	Abc
	Q4	Abc
2011	Q1	Abc
	Q2	Abc
	Q3	Abc
	Q4	Abc
2012	Q1	Abc
	Q2	Abc
	Q3	Abc
	Q4	Abc

Let's walk through the datepart version first. In this case, the quarter is really Q1, Q2, Q3, Q4:

1. There are four addressing partitions for Q1, Q2, Q3, Q4.
2. There are 15 addresses since 2009 as Q3 has been filtered out.
3. The addressing partition addresses with the ranking position number are as follows:

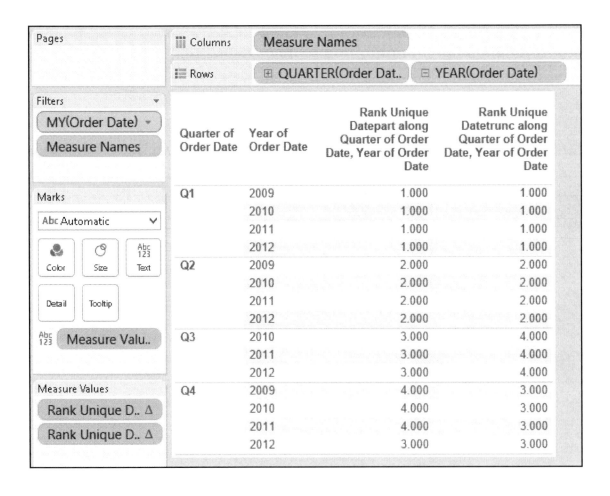

4. The ranking partition is as follows:

Quarter of Order Date	Year of Order Date	Rank Unique Datepart along Quarter of Order Date, Year of Order Date
Q1	2009	1.000
	2010	2.000
	2011	3.000
	2012	4.000
Q2	2009	1.000
	2010	2.000
	2011	3.000
	2012	4.000
Q3	2010	1.000
	2011	2.000
	2012	3.000
Q4	2009	1.000
	2010	2.000
	2011	3.000
	2012	4.000

5. The ranking partitions are sorted by the measure in the RANK_UNIQUE function; in this case, it is DATEPART('quarter',MIN([Order Date])). It does not change anything from step 4.

6. The ranking is applied to each ranking partition. The result is as follows:

Rank Unique Datepart	Quarter of Order Date	Year of Order Date
1	Q1	2009
	Q2	2009
	Q3	2010
	Q4	2009
2	Q1	2010
	Q2	2010
	Q3	2011
	Q4	2010
3	Q1	2011
	Q2	2011
	Q3	2012
	Q4	2011
4	Q1	2012
	Q2	2012
	Q4	2012

For the DATETRUNC example, the first 4 steps are the same as the DATEPART in the view. So let's start with step 5:

7. The ranking partitions are sorted by the measure; in this case, it is
`DATETRUNC('quarter', MIN([Order Date]))`. The sort is different from
datapart since instead of sorting on just Quarter, it is sorting on Year and Quarter.
The result is as follows:

Rank Unique Datepart	Quarter of Order Date	Year of Order Date	Rank Unique Datepart along Quarter of Order Date, Year of Order Date
1	Q1	2009	1.000
	Q2	2009	2.000
	Q3	2010	3.000
	Q4	2009	4.000
2	Q1	2010	1.000
	Q2	2010	2.000
	Q3	2011	3.000
	Q4	2010	4.000
3	Q1	2011	1.000
	Q2	2011	2.000
	Q3	2012	3.000
	Q4	2011	4.000
4	Q1	2012	1.000
	Q2	2012	2.000
	Q4	2012	3.000

8. The rank is applied to each ranking partition. The result is as follows:

Rank Unique Datepart	Quarter of Order Date (Quarters)	Quarter of Order Date	Year of Order Date
1	2009 Q1	Q1	2009
	2009 Q2	Q2	2009
	2009 Q4	Q4	2009
	2010 Q3	Q3	2010
2	2010 Q1	Q1	2010
	2010 Q2	Q2	2010
	2010 Q4	Q4	2010
	2011 Q3	Q3	2011
3	2011 Q1	Q1	2011
	2011 Q2	Q2	2011
	2011 Q4	Q4	2011
	2012 Q3	Q3	2012
4	2012 Q1	Q1	2012
	2012 Q2	Q2	2012
	2012 Q4	Q4	2012

Example 5:

In the preceding Rank Datepart example, the Rank for Q4 2009 is 4:

Rank Unique Datepart	Quarter of Order Date	Year of Order Date
1	Q1	2009
	Q2	2009
	Q3	2010
	Q4	2009
2	Q1	2010
	Q2	2010
	Q3	2011
	Q4	2010
3	Q1	2011
	Q2	2011
	Q3	2012
	Q4	2011
4	Q1	2012
	Q2	2012
	Q4	2012

If I change the layout to crosstab with quarter on rows and year on columns, the Q4 2009 gets a rank of 3. The result is as follows:

Rank Unique Datepart	Quarter of Order Date (Quarters)	Quarter of Order Date	Year of Order Date	Rank Unique Datetrunc along Quarter of Order Date, Year of Order Date, Quarter of Order Date (Quarte..
1	2009 Q1	Q1	2009	1.000
	2009 Q2	Q2	2009	2.000
	2009 Q4	Q4	2009	3.000
	2010 Q3	Q3	2010	4.000
2	2010 Q1	Q1	2010	1.000
	2010 Q2	Q2	2010	2.000
	2010 Q4	Q4	2010	3.000
	2011 Q3	Q3	2011	4.000
3	2011 Q1	Q1	2011	1.000
	2011 Q2	Q2	2011	2.000
	2011 Q4	Q4	2011	3.000
	2012 Q3	Q3	2012	4.000
4	2012 Q1	Q1	2012	1.000
	2012 Q2	Q2	2012	2.000
	2012 Q4	Q4	2012	3.000

The reason is that domain padding. In the original Datepart tank example, there are 15 marks. In the crosstab example, there are 16 marks, and Tableau is adding the missing mark for Q3 2009 using domain padding. If you right-click to view data, you will see Tableau add null value for Q3 2009:

Rank Unique Datepart	Quarter of Order Date	Year of Order Date	Rank Unique Datepart along Quarter of Order Date, Year of Order Date
1	Q1	2009	1.000
	Q2	2009	2.000
	Q3	2010	3.000
	Q4	2009	4.000
2	Q1	2010	1.000
	Q2	2010	2.000
	Q3	2011	3.000
	Q4	2010	4.000
3	Q1	2011	1.000
	Q2	2011	2.000
	Q3	2012	3.000
	Q4	2011	4.000
4	Q1	2012	1.000
	Q2	2012	2.000
	Q4	2012	3.000

These are the steps that Tableau performs to calculate the results:

1. There are four addressing partitions for Q1, Q2, Q3, Q4.
2. There are 16 addresses in the view because even though Q3 2009 has been filtered out, it has been padded back in by domain padding.

3. The addressing partition addresses with the ordinal position number are as follows. Note that 2010 Q3 gets the third position even though it doesn't exist in the underlying data; it's only from the padding that it exists:

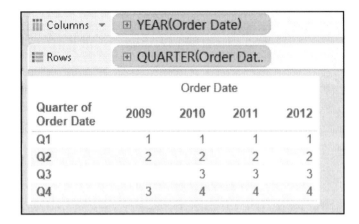

4. Each year has a ranking partition.
5. Tableau sorts the partition based on the measure. In this case, it is `DATEPART('quarter',MIN([Order Date]))`. However, the `MIN([Order Date])` for Q3 2009 does not exist in the data, so it returns Null (even in the padded data), which changes the sort.
6. Then the RANK_UNIQUE function is applied. Since the RANK calculation ignores Nulls, `RANK_UNIQUE` returns Null for Q3 2009.

To prevent unwanted domain completion, you can put all your addressing dimensions on the level of detail shelf and use discrete measures, such as `ATTR(AddressingDimension)`, to generate proper headers. For example, put Date on the Detail Shelf, and put `ATTR(Year)` and `ATTR(Month)` on column/row to be headers.

LOD calculations

In the previous section, we talked about table calculation. LOD calculation is another important calculation type. LOD calculation is a fairly new feature in Tableau, starting to available in Tableau 9. But it is essential in many forms of data analytics.

Overview

LOD calculation stands for level of detail calculation. LOD expressions give you the flexibility to calculate the aggregated results that are not on the same level of detail in the view. For example, you may want to know the biggest deal closed by each rep but only show the sum of those deals by manager in the view. This can be achieved using LOD calculation.

Key Concepts

The key concept to understand LOD calculation is to understand level of detail. For example, in the Superstore data source orders table, we have the lowest level for sales as per order ID per product. But we may want to see the aggregated sales per product category.

In Tableau, the way to define level of detail is to drag and drop the dimensions into the view. Any dimension that is on the columns, rows, color, size, label, detail, and path will change the level of detail. Any dimension that is on pages, filters, and tooltip will not change the level of detail.

Since the level of detail for a visualization is defined by the dimensions in the viz, you cannot aggregate your measures to the level of detail based on other dimensions that are not in the Viz. But LOD calculations allow you to do that.

LOD Functions

There are three types of LOD calculations: EXCLUDE, INCLUDE, and FIXED.

- EXCLUDE: It is used to exclude the dimension that is in the view. The result is calculated based on the dimensions in the view minus the dimension specified in the LOD calculation.
- INCLUDE: It is used to include the dimension that is not in the view. The result is calculated based on the dimension specified in the LOD calculation plus all the dimensions in the view.
- FIXED: It is used to define the specific dimension without referring to any dimension in the view. The result is calculated only based on the dimension specified in the LOD calculation. FIXED also ignores any filter in the view except context filter, data source filter, and extract filter.

LOD Use Cases

LOD Remix

I assume you already know the basic use cases of each LOD calculation, that is, Fixed, Include, and Exclude. In this section, we are going to walk through an example of how to pick the right LOD calculation based on your use case.

I will use the Superstore data set for this example. In the Superstore data set, there are multiple Product Sub-Categories for each Region. The goal is to find the largest Product Sub-Category for each Region based on number of orders. The steps are as follows:

1. Drag Region to the view on Rows.
2. Create a calculated field called No of Orders as COUNTD([Order ID])

    Before we start working on the LOD calculation, there are a few key points to pay attention to:

    - FIXED LOD calculations have only the dimensions specified in the LOD calculation.
    - INCLUDE & EXCLUDE LOD calculations use both the specified dimensions and any dimensions in the view. If the LOD calculation is nested inside one another, the inner calculation includes/excludes dimensions from the outer expressions.
    - Regular dimension filters will apply after FIXED LOD calculation but before INCLUDE & EXCLUDE LOD expressions. So the default for FIXED LOD expressions is that they are computed across all the data. To filter dimensions prior to computation of FIXED LOD expressions, we have to use context filters.

3. Create an LOD calculation to get the number of orders for each region/product sub-category {FIXED [Region],[Product Sub-Category]:[No of Orders]}.
4. Create an LOD calculation to get the maximum number of region/product sub-category orders for each region {FIXED [Region]:MAX([Region Category Orders])}.
5. Create a calculation to get the Product Sub-Category with the maximum number of orders: if [Region Category Orders]=[Max Region Orders], then [Product Sub-Category] END.

This is what the view looks like:

It shows the Product Sub-Category for each region with the biggest number of orders.

I used FIXED LOD calculation for this example because I feel it is easy, and you do not need to worry about the dimensions you have in the view. But you can achieve the same goal with other types of LOD calculations.

LOD and Totals

You may wonder how Tableau calculates totals for LOD calculations. To understand that, let's first talk about the totals in Tableau. In Tableau, there are two types of totals: one is Totals (aka single-pass totals) and the other is Visual Totals (aka two-pass totals). Totals (aka single-pass totals) is the default setting when you turn on Totals in Analytics. This option appears in the Total Using menu as "Automatic".

Let's look at an example of single-pass Totals. In the following example, you can see that subtotals are SUM(Sales) per Product Category, and Grand Total is the SUM(Sales) for the entire table:

	Order Date			
Quarter of Order Date	2009	2010	2011	2012
Q1	1	2	3	4
Q2	1	2	3	4
Q3	1	2	3	4
Q4	1	2	3	4

If you want the Total to show the AVG value instead of SUM, you will need to use the Visual Totals (aka two-pass totals). You can change the Visual Totals by changing the "Total Using" from Automatic to AVG, as shown in the following screenshot:

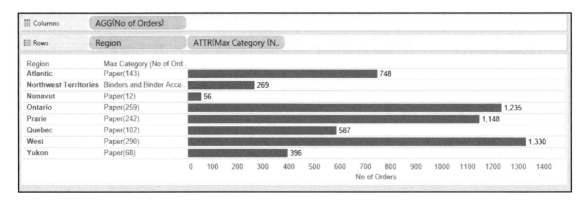

Now let's talk about the totals for LOD calculations. Actually, the totals work exactly the same for LOD calculations. For example, you have Product Category in your view but your LOD calculation is {INCLUDE [Product Sub-Category]:SUM([Sales])}. Tableau will calculate the total for Product Category, Product Sub-Category levels. Total calculation only changes when you set the Compute Using. The following is the default Automatic Compute Using setting, so it is total using SUM:

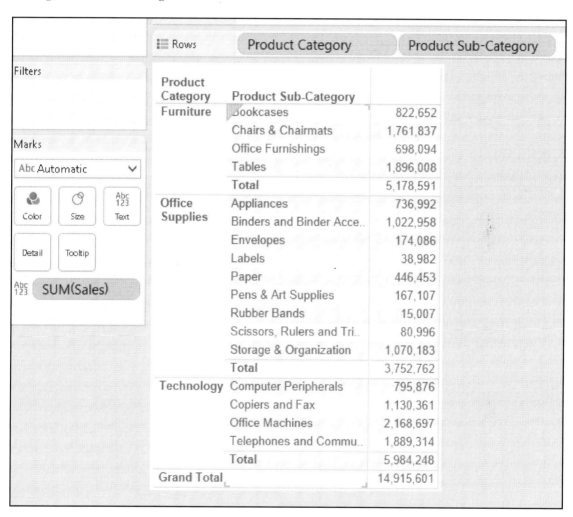

If I change the Compute Using option to AVG, you will see that Tableau is calculating the AVG value for Product Category, Product Sub-Category level SUM (Sales):

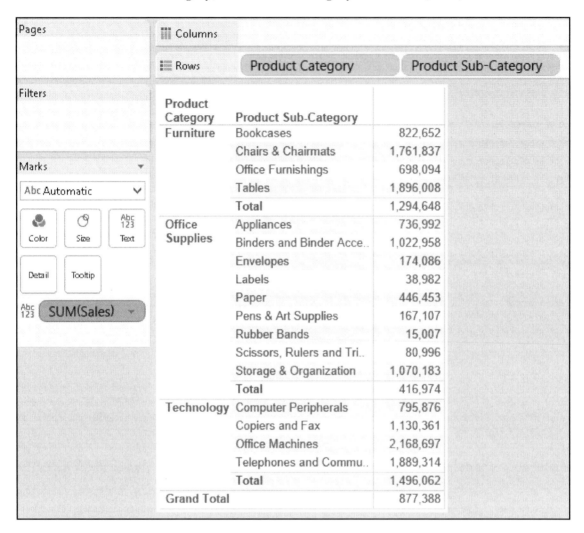

LOD nesting

You can nest many layers of LOD calculations to answer even more complex business questions. One thing to keep in mind is that the context for a calculation is defined by its parent(s) as opposed to the sheet. For example, {FIXED[Product Category] : AVG({INCLUDE[Customer Name] : SUM([Sales])})} is the same as {FIXED [Product Category] : AVG({FIXED [Product Category], [Customer Name] : SUM([Sales])})}. Since nested calculation inherits the dimension from the outer calculation, in the first case, result in the level of detail is Product Category ,Customer Name. Also since outer calculation is fixed, nested calculation will not be affected by the filters in the sheet.

Now let's look at another example in which you are trying to calculate the average customer sales for each region, but you feel that customers who travel and spend a small amount of money in multiple regions are affecting the results. Instead of filtering them out, you want to calculate the total sales for each customer and then calculate average on region. You can do it as {FIXED [Region], [Customer Name] : AVG({EXCLUDE [Region] : SUM([Sales])})}.

In this example, Tableau will first calculate the Sum of Sales for each Customer Name. Since the outer aggregation is by Region, Customer, it will result in the replication of the total sales for each customer for each state in which the customer made a purchase.

The below shows the Sum of Sales for each customer. When adding region, the sum of sales for each customer is replicated.

When you drag the calculation to the view as aggregated on AVG, you will see the result as follows:

The final result is the average of the total customer sales for each state. The (AVG({EXLUDE [Region] : ….) does not do anything. The average happens in the view when you set the calculation to be aggregated as AVG.

LOD limitations

There are the following limitations to keep in mind when using LOD calculations:

- Sets, combined fields, parameters, and table calculations cannot be used in the dimensionality expression.

- Only field names can be used in the dimension expression (for example, an expression like MAX([Order Date]) or YEAR([Order Date]) or an IF statement cannot be used in the dimension expression). But you can use a calculated field that has the formula YEAR([Order Date]) and use that instead. If you use {EXCLUDE [Order Date] : SUM([Sales])} and have [Order Date] in your sheet, Tableau will recognize the date hierarchy and automatically exclude the dateparts from the calculation's level of detail as you drill down.

- Table calculations and ATTR are not allowed in aggregate expression; for example, {FIXED [Region] : ATTR([Product Category])} or {Fixed [Region] : INDEX()} are not supported.

- Dimension from one source with measure from another blended source cannot be mixed in an LOD calculation.

- All dimensions in the dimension expression should come from the same data source.

- LOD expressions that use exclude or include keywords cannot be used as dimensions. They also cannot be binned. This is because they have relative dimensions. While this may appear like an arbitrary limitation, it makes them much more understandable. Consider the case where there are two include calculations in the sheet, and they are used as dimensions. Calculation1 is {INCLUDE A : MIN(a)}, Calculation2 is {INCLUDE B : MIN(b)}. If there are no other dimensions in the sheet, Calculation1 will behave like {FIXED A, Calculation2 : MIN(a)}, and Calculation2 will behave like {FIXED B, Calculation1 : MIN(b)}. Circular reference!

- LOD calculations from secondary sources cannot be used via data blending.

Date calculations

In the previous section, we talked about LOD calculations. Now let's look at some examples of Date calculations.

Using Date Tableau calculation to hide parts of the date

This is a small yet very useful trick when you want to hide part of the date without affecting other parts of the Viz. In the example, we want to show the running total of the sales for all time, but we only want to show a particular date range in the Viz.

If you use the date filter, the running total will only be calculated based on the date range in your filter, not all time. But we have a solution using the table calculation on Date. I will use the Superstore data for this example. The following are the steps to be performed:

1. Drag Order Date to Columns as Month.
2. Drag Sales to Rows as SUM.
3. Do a quick table calculation on Sales using Running Total. Now you see the view as follows:

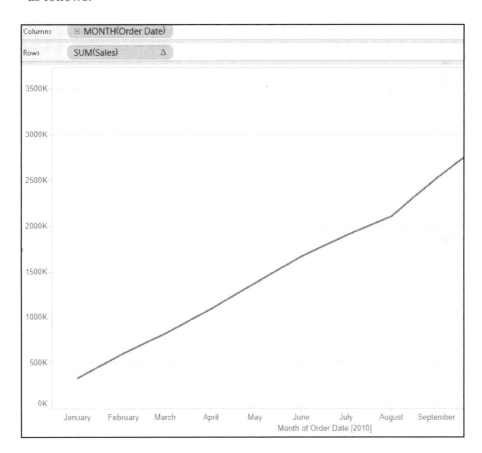

4. If I want to see only the data in 2010, and I use date as the filter, the Running Total starts from 0:

5. Create two date parameters: one as Start Date and another as End Date.

6. Create a customer date. Since I am showing the data as monthly, I will create a custom date for month:

7. What we really want to do is filter out the date range in the Viz, not from the underlying data that Tableau is using to calculate the numbers in the Viz. To achieve this goal, we will create a calculated field, as follows:

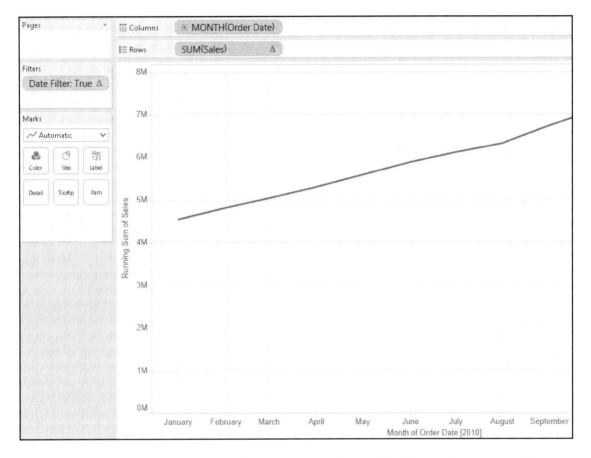

- The goal of this lookup function is to tell Tableau that we are only interested in the position of the date in the view, not the underlying data. So Tableau will make sure that each point that is showing in the view is between the date range of the two date parameters.

8. Drag the Date filter to the view and choose "True". Now you will see the filtered view, as follows:

```
MID(LEFT([UserEmail],FIND([UserEmail],"@")-1), FIND([UserEmail],".")+1)
```

- The view is showing the Running Total of the Sales for 2010, which starts from the beginning of Year Running Total in 2010 instead of 0.

String calculations

In the previous section, we talked about Date calculation. In this section, we will learn about String calculations.

Getting last name from an email

A lot of times we need to get the last name out of an email. A simple String calculation will do the work.

For example, if I want to get last name from an email address like firstName.lastname@example.com. The calculation is as follows:

Customer Name	Product
Go	Shrimp
MJ	Shrimp
Go	Crab
Ken	Fish
MJ	Fish

You can get the string on the left of the "@" using the LEFT function. The next step is to use the MID function to get the string from the period to the left of the "@".

Getting street number from address

For example, I want to get the street number from the first line of an address, which includes the characters from the beginning until the first space. The calculation is as follows:

LEFT(LTRIM([StreetAddress]), FIND(LTRIM([StreetAddress]+" ")," ") -1)

LTRIM(string) removes leading blank spaces, FIND(LTRIM([StreetAddress]+" ")," ") returns the position of the first blank, and LEFT(string, n) returns the first n characters of the string, that is, all the characters left to the first blank. A blank is added to the first parameter of the FIND statement to ensure that the calculation works if the string contains only one word.

Counting number of words in a string

Let's say I want to get the number of words in some text that are separated by space. The calculation is as follows:

LEN(TRIM([Text]))-LEN(REPLACE(TRIM([Text])," ",""))+1

The purpose of REPLACE is to remove all the blanks. To remove blanks at the beginning and the end, you can use the TRIM function. After removing extra blanks, the words in the text are separated by one blank.

Count

Total for count distinct

Count Distinct returns the number of unique values in a field. But when you use Count Distinct with subtotals or grand totals, you may not always get the result you want.

For example, you have a simple set of data, as follows:

Customer Name	Product
Go	Shrimp
MJ	Shrimp
Go	Crab
Ken	Fish
MJ	Fish

You want to know the number of unique products bought by each customer and then understand the total number of unique products bought by all customers. In Tableau, your initial view may look like the following screenshot:

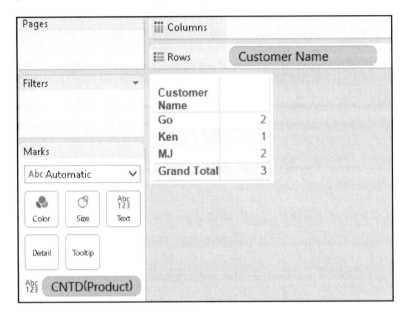

You want to see the total the number of unique products per customer, so the number you want is five. However, Tableau is calculating the count distinct of product, so it is showing three: crab, fish, and shrimp.

The solution is as follows:

1. Created a calculated field with the name Customer Name and Product; the calculation is [Customer Name]+[Product].
2. The new calculation calculates each unique combination of Customer Names and Product. For each Customer Name, the Count Distinct is still the same, but for the total, the Count Distinct treats shrimp bought by Go as a different (distinct) product from shrimp bought by MJ.
3. Drag Customer Name and Product to Text to replace Product.
4. Right-click on Customer Name and Product, and choose Measure > Count (Distinct).

The view is like the following screenshot:

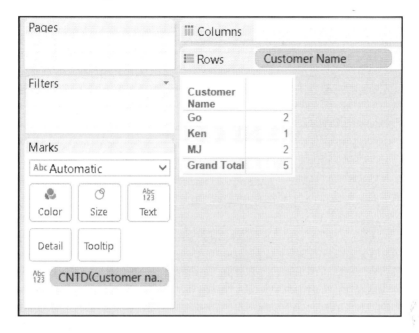

Alternatives for count distinct

Count Distinct is very important to analytics. But it requires a lot of calculations, and the performance can be very bad. The performance will be even worse on large data sets. But you have some other to get the same result as using count distinct, which are as follows:

1. Visualization trick: First put your dimension onto the Detail shelf. Then put the Number of Records onto Rows, and change it to Maximum (or Min, Avg). This way, you can get a bar chart with small bars stacked to each other. The total of the stacked bars is the same as count distinct.

2. Size(): The table calculation "SIZE()" function can calculate the number of rows in a partition. Put a calculated field using Size() and into the view, and set the Compute Using as the your Dimension, you can get the same result as count distinct.

3. Data blending: First you need to have a data source where there is only one row for each instance of the Dimension. Blend this data source with the original data source, and the number of records in the secondary source is the same as the count distinct.

Data blending limitation with COUNTD

Data blending has some limitations regarding non-additive aggregates, such as COUNTD, MEDIAN, and RAWSQLAGG. These limitations cause certain fields in the view to become invalid in certain circumstances. If you hover your mouse cursor over one of these fields, the error is: "Cannot blend the secondary data source because one or more fields use an unsupported aggregation."

The limitations are as follows:

- If a non-additive aggregation from the primary data source is in the view, you cannot use a group created in the primary data source in the view. As a workaround, you can change the group into a calculated field.
- Non-additive aggregates are only supported for the primary data source if that data source is a relational data source that allows the use of temporary tables. Non-additive aggregates are not supported for any secondary data sources. If you need a non-additive aggregate on the primary data source, but your data source does not support temporary tables, you can create an extract. Tableau data extracts support temporary tables. If you are using a secondary dimension, try changing the dimension to an attribute. However, using Attribute might replace values with an asterisk (*), which means that there are multiple values in your data at this level of detail, and Tableau can't determine which to display.

Custom Total

Custom Grand Total

I will use the Superstore data set for this example.

For example, you want to get the sum of the average sales for each customer segment in the Grand Total row. But what you are getting now is the overall average of the data source, which is as follows:

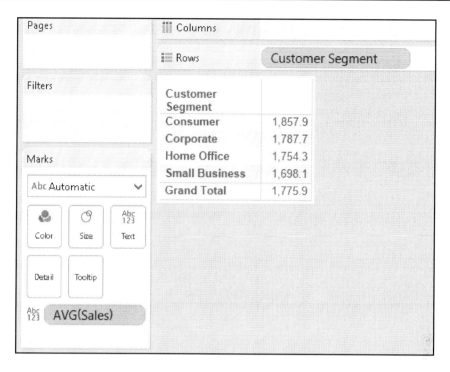

How is Tableau calculating the Grand Total? It is performing the same calculation for the measure as it does for the Dimension in the view, but at a higher level. In this case, the entire data source is considered instead of each customer segment. Tableau uses all the dimensions on the columns to calculate column Grand Total. Same goes for row Grand Total.

In the example, the AVG (Sales) for each Customer Segment is calculated first. Then to calculate the Grand Total, since there is no dimension on the column, Tableau calculates AVG (Sales) using the entire data source.

To customize the Grand Total, the following methods can be used:

- Understand how grand total is calculated
- Create the calculation that returns the desired value for the Grand Total

The key to understanding the Grand Total is to figure out which dimensions are used to calculate the Grand Total. In the aforementioned example, since there is no dimension on the column, no dimension is used to calculate the Grand Total. So Tableau uses all the data to calculate the Grand Total.

We can create the following calculation to get our desired Grand Total:

IF MIN ([Customer Segment])! = MAX ([Customer Segment]) THEN

SUM ([Sales]) ELSE AVG ([Sales])

END

This technique has the following limitations:

- MIN () and MAX () will return one dimension. The calculation can fail if a hierarchy is used. But you can use parameters and calculated fields to control the dimensions in the view and the calculations.
- Only an aggregate result will be returned. The goal of this example is to get the sum of the average of sales per Customer Segment, which means aggregating the average sales for each customer segment to sum.

Another Way of Custom Grand Total

Since the desired Grand Total is SUM of AVG, we can use the table calculation WINDOW_SUM (AVG ([Sales])).

The result for each Customer Segment is the same using Table (Down), but the Grand Total shows the result for the entire data. In order to get the Grand Total we want, Customer Segment needs to be used in the level of detail for Grand Total.

The solution is to duplicate customer segment and put it on the level of detail shelf. The Compute Using is Customer Segment (copy).

There are some limitations, as follows:

- Tableau is calculating the result for each value of Customer Segment (copy). Since Customer Segment and Customer Segment (copy) have the same values, the WINDOW_SUM (AVG ([Sales])) function just returns the AVG ([Sales]).
- The calculation of Grand Total is performed for each value of Customer Segment (copy), so we get four results in Grand Total, as follows:

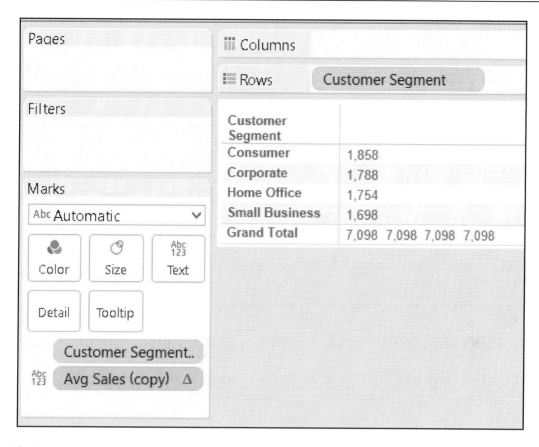

To fix this, we update our calculation to the following:

IF FIRST () = =0 THEN WINDOW_SUM (AVG ([Sales]), 0, IIF (FIRST () = =0, LAST (), 0))

END

The result is as follows:

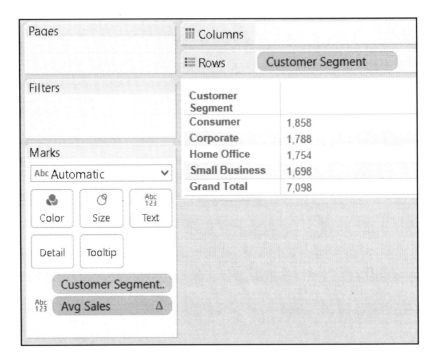

Dynamic parameter

The idea of dynamic parameter is to create a string type parameter with the list of strings to be able to change dynamically when the underlying data source is changing. A solution is to use Custom SQL.

First, create a Custom SQL query like the following:

(This is in general terms)

Select [Your Dimension]

From [Your Datasource]

Group by [Your Dimension]

The query will return all the values in the dimension, and it will dynamically change when the underlying data changes.

Summary

In summary, you should keep in mind the following best practices for calculation.

You should choose the right partition and addressing dimensions for your table calculation; you can test with a small set of data when you feel confused. One way that works for me to figure out the partition and addressing for my table calculation is that I put all my dimensions to the addressing dimensions of advanced table calculation box, while the sequence of the addressing dimensions in the table calculation box is from top to bottom as it is from left to right in the view.

You should know how Tableau is calculating Rank (). Sometimes it could be very confusing. You need to understand the difference of DATEPART and DATETRUC in table calculations.

You must choose the right level for your LOD calculation based on your use case. I prefer to use Fixed over the other two since I do not need to worry about the dimensions in the view. You should keep in mind the limitations for COUNTD. You should use table calculations to customize the total for your use case.

In the next chapter, we will talk about how to use Sort/Filter to make your view more intuitive for the users to see and limit the data in the view based on your analytics needs.

4
Sort and Filter

In the previous chapter, we talked about how to use different types of calculation parameters, focusing on table calculations and LOD calculations since they are the most confusing ones. In this chapter, we will talk about how to use sort/filter to make the **View** more intuitive for the users and limit the data in the **View** based on your analytics needs. In this chapter, we will cover the following:

- Different types of sorting
- Sorting by calculated field
- Different types of filters
- Filter operation order
- Filtering by calculated field
- Compare filter, group, and set
- Cascading filter
- Dynamic set/filter

Different types of sorting

Two different ways of sorting are available in Tableau:

- The first option is to sort by clicking on the dimension in **View** and then clicking on **Sort**. It is very easy to use, but you cannot use this in table calculations.
- The second option is to add the calculation that you want the sorting to be based on to the left of the dimension you want to sort.

You cannot sort calculations or fields from a secondary data source.

Sort by calculated field

If you want to sort a table calculation, you need to have a copy of the same table calculation and set it as discrete. You can drag the copy of the table calculation to **View** as the first dimension in **Rows/Columns**. The **View** will be sorted by the table calculation.

Let's look at an example. I will use the Superstore data for this example.

The goals for this visualization are as follows:

1. Show the latest sales and sales trend for each **Province**.
2. Sort the three strategic provinces (**Quebec**, **Ontario**, and **Alberta**) by the latest sales. Other provinces are sorted alphabetically.

Here are the steps to create this visualization:

1. Drag **Order Date** to columns and set as **Month**.
2. Drag **Province** to **Rows**.
3. Drag **Measure Names** to **Rows**.
4. Drag **Measure Values** to **Text**.
5. Set **Measure Names** as filter and keep **Sales only**. You will get a simple table, as follows:

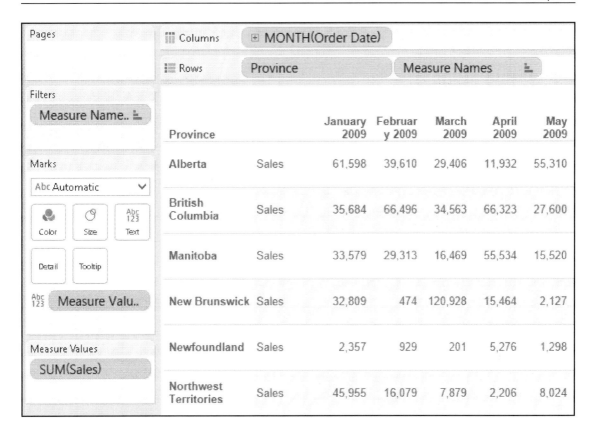

6. Create a table calculation to get the `Latest Sales` value:

Latest Sales   Orders (Sample - Superstore Sales (Excel))

Results are computed along Table (Across).
WINDOW_MAX(IIF(LAST()=0,LOOKUP(SUM([Sales]),0),null))|

7. Drag **Latest Sales** to **Measure Values**, and set **Compute using** as **Table (Across)**. You will see that it is showing the **Latest Sales** values for each **Province**, as shown next:

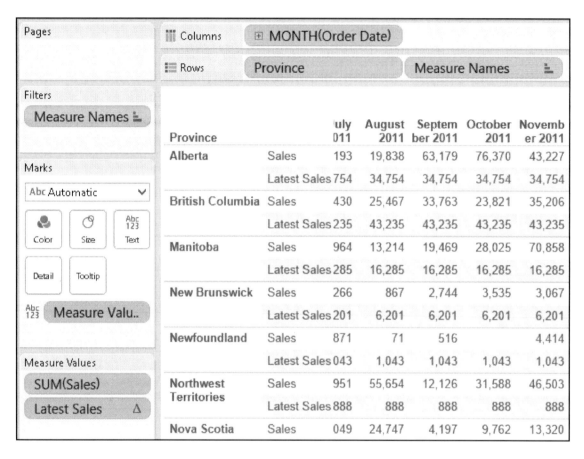

8. Change **Latest Sales** to discrete and move to **Rows**.
9. Change **Order Date** to **continuous**.

10. Move **Sales** to **Rows**.

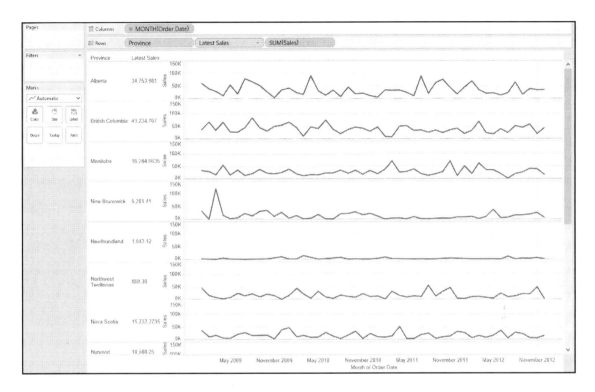

11. Now let's focus on the sorting. We want to sort the three strategic provinces (**Quebec**, **Ontario**, **Alberta**) by **Latest Sales** in a descending order, followed by all of the remaining provinces in alphabetical order. If you look at the sort options for **Province**, **Latest Sales** is not one of the options. That's because **Latest Sales** is a table calculation and table calculations are not available for sorting. I can create some table calculations that will make the sorting work. I can create one **calculated field** to do it, but it is better to create separate calculations so I can reuse them. The first calculation is the `Negative Latest Sales` and also converts nulls to zeros. Set **Compute using** to **Order Date**.

12. Drag **Negative Latest Sales** to **Rows**, and change it to **discrete**:

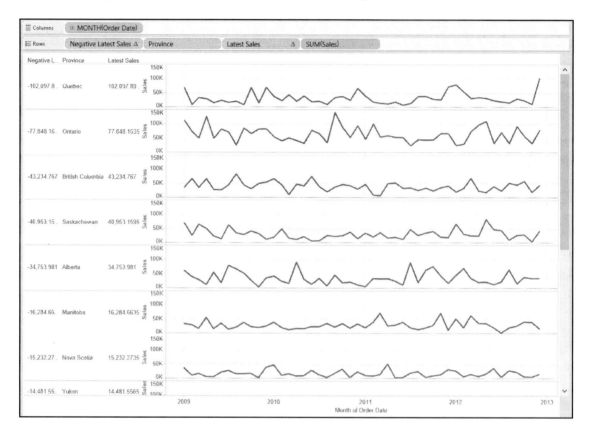

13. All the provinces are now sorted by **Latest Sales** in a descending order. Now I need to apply sorting only to the three strategic provinces (**Quebec**, **Ontario**, and **Alberta**). I create another **calculated field** to do that. It looks like this:

```
Province Sort                    Orders (Sample - Superstore Sales (Excel))

Results are computed along Table (Across).
if
ATTR([Province])="Quebec"
or
ATTR([Province])="Ontario"
OR
ATTR([Province])="Alberta"
then [Negative Latest Sales]
ELSE WINDOW_MAX(MAX(0))
END
```

14. Drag the **Province Sort** calculation to **Rows**, change it to **discrete**, and replace **Negative Latest Sales**. You will see that the three strategic provinces, which are sorted by **Latest Sales**, are in descending order, and the rest are sorted alphabetically:

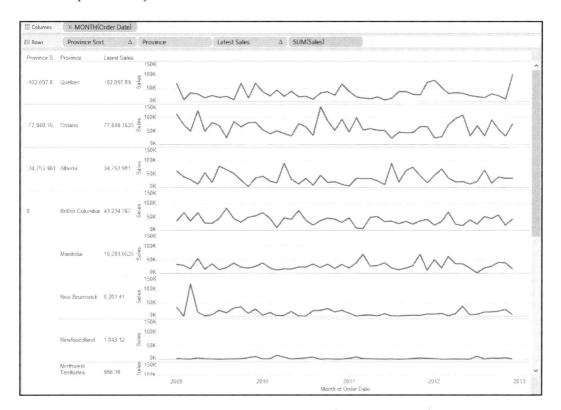

15. Now let's clean up **Viz** to make it look better:
    1. Hide the header of **Province Sort**.
    2. Change the format of **Latest Sales** to **Currency**.
    3. Edit the **Sales** axis: Change **Range** to **independent**, and uncheck **Include zero**.
    4. Hide the header for the **Sales** axis.
    5. Make the row headers bold.
    6. Remove the title from the **Order Date** axis.
    7. Add a fake header for **Sales**.
    8. Add a three-month moving average of sales
    9. Filter the **View** to keep **Order Date** of 2011 and 2012.

The final view looks as follows:

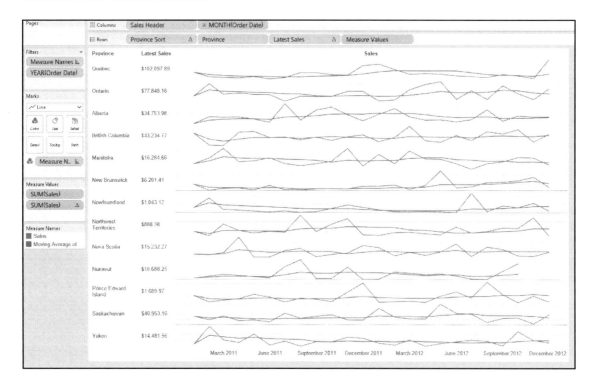

Different types of filters

There are the following three four types of filters in Tableau:

Custom SQL: Adding where in the SQL that will be used in the tableau

- **Data source filters**: Adding filters after loading the data – to restrict the data to be visible to the users.
- **Extract filters**: Created when we create extract based on the data we get after using data source filters.
- **Context filters**: added inside the worksheet
- **Traditional filters**: dragging dim and measures in the worksheet in the filter box

You can use these filters to control what data to show in the visualization. Let's walk through them one by one.

Data source filter

A data source filter is like the WHERE clause in SQL, which is used to extract data. It isnormally used to control the size of the data extract. Reducing the size of the extract can speed up the load of your **Viz**.

You can create a data source filter after extracting the data; then right-click on **data extract** and select **Edit data source filters**, as shown next:

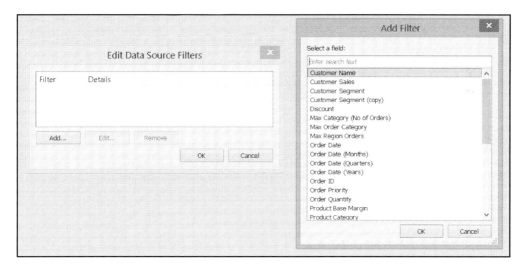

Context filter

A context filter is used to limit the data that is used in the worksheets. When Tableau is querying the data from the data source to load into the worksheet, it creates a temp table to keep the data. All the data that is removed by a data source filter or context filter will not go into the temp table. The purpose of context filter is also to control the size of the temp table and keep only the minimum amount of the data you need for your **Viz**.

Context filters are better than traditional filters in certain ways. First, they are executed much faster than and run before traditional filters. They can also be run at once. The bad thing is that it is time-consuming for the filter to be placed into context. The golden rule is that if a context filter cannot reduce the data by over 10%, do not put it as a context filter.

You can create a context filter by simply dragging a field onto the **Filters** shelf, then clicking on **field** and choosing **Add to context**. If you need more than one context filter, you can use Ctrl to select all the fields and then add them to context together. But keep in mind that too many context filters can have a negative impact on the performance, so do not add a field to context if it cannot reduce the data size by over 10%.

Another thing to keep in mind about context filter is that the LOD calculation is done after the context filter is applied. You can actually take advantage of this fact to build a certain **Viz** for your needs.

Traditional filter

A traditional filter is probably the most commonly used filter. Normally, when people talk about filters in Tableau, they are thinking about traditional filters. Tableau removes value that is filtered out by traditional filters when creating the visualization. It is the slowest of all filter types. But it can perform some complex filtering, such as the **Top N** filters. You can create a traditional filter by simply dragging a field onto the **Filters** shelf.

Filter order

If you implement different types of filters in your workbooks, it is important to remember the order in which Tableau executes those filters so you can get the results you are expecting; the order is as follows:

1. Extract filters.
2. Data source filters.
3. Context filters.

4. Filters on dimensions (whether on the **Filters** shelf or in filter cards in **View**).

5. Filters on measures (whether on the **Filters** shelf or in filter cards in **View**).

Filtering by calculated fields

In the previous section, we talked about different types of filters. In this section, we will focus on discussing different use cases of filtering by calculated fields.

Top N Rank

Now let's look at an example of using `Rank()` table calculation to filter the top product sub-categories for each order year in the Superstore data set.

1. Drag **Order Date** to **Rows**, and set as **Year (Order Date)**.

2. Drag **Product Sub-Category** to **Rows**.

3. Drag **SUM (Sales)** to **Columns**. You will see the following:

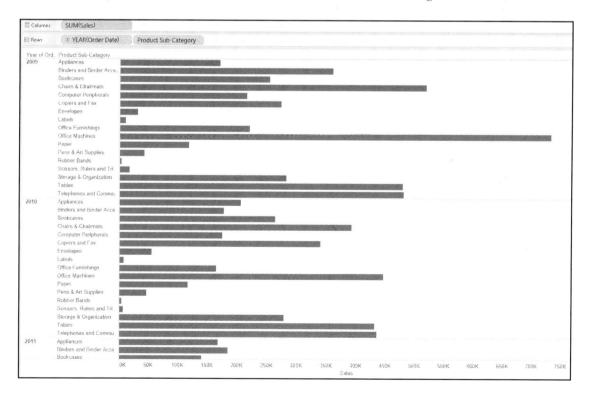

4. The goal is to look at the top five product sub-categories for each order year, based on sales. To achieve this goal, we duplicate **SUM (Sales)** by dragging while pressing Ctrl. Then we create a quick table calculation of `Rank()`, set **Compute using** as **Product Sub-Category**.

5. Set **Product Sub-Category** to sort based on **SUM (Sales)**. You will see the following:

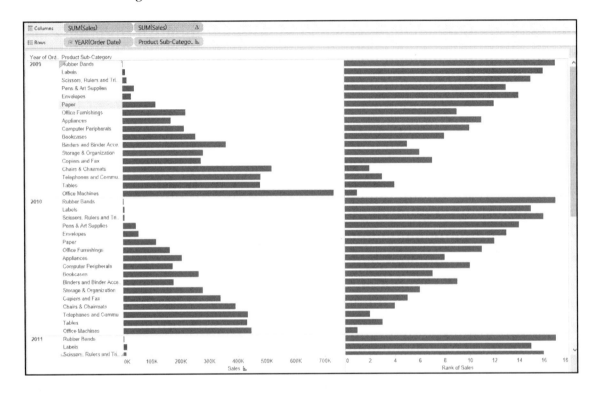

6. Change the table calculation of **SUM (Sales)** to discrete and drag it to **Rows** in between **YEAR (Order Date)** and **Product Sub-Category**. Now you can see that for each order year, the **Product Sub-Category** is sorted by **SUM (Sales)**.

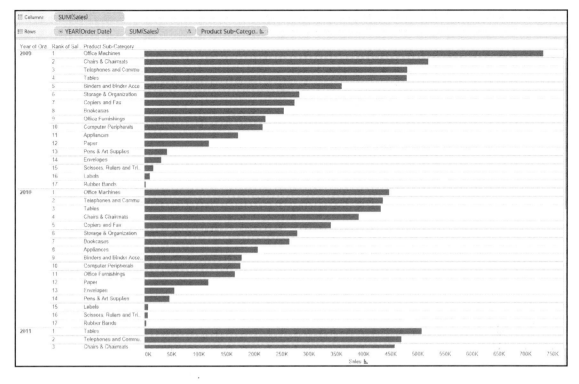

7. Since we only want to see the top five sales in **Product Sub-Category** for each order year, we can use the **Rank SUM (Sales)** table calculation as a filter. Change **SUM(Sales)** to **continuous** and keep the range of **1-5**.

8. Hide the **SUM (Sales)** table calculation from **View**. You will see the following:

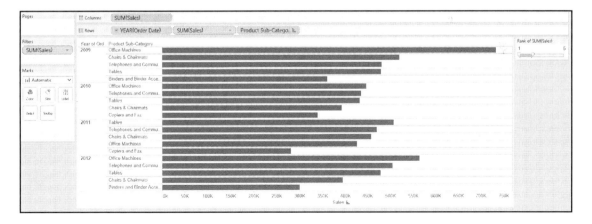

Top and bottom percentage

Now let's look at another example of using table calculation to filter the top/bottom *N*% customers based on profit in the Superstore data set. The following steps need to be performed:

1. Drag **Customer Name** to **Rows**.
2. Drag **SUM (Profit)** to **Columns**.
3. Sort **Customer Name** by **Profit** in a descending order.
4. Drag **SUM (Profit)** to the color shelf.

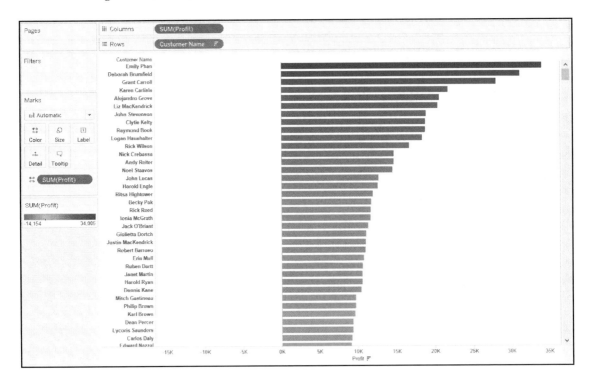

5. Create a **calculated field** called `Number of Customers` using `size ()`.

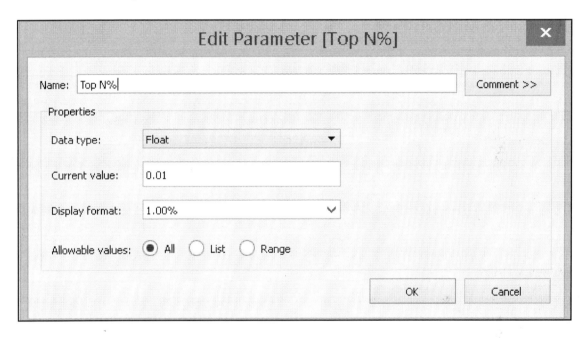

6. Create a parameter called `Top N%`.

7. Create another **calculated field** using the `Number of Customers` field to get the `Top and Bottom N% customers`, as follows:

8. Drag **Top and Bottom N% Customers** to the **Filter** shelf, and select **True**.
9. Create another **calculated field** as the header.

```
Top and Bottom N% Customer          Orders (Sample - Superstore Sales (Excel))

Results are computed along Table (Across).
if INDEX()<=[Number of Customers]*[Top N%]
then "Top "+STR([Top N%]*100)+"%"
elseif  INDEX()>=[Number of Customers]*(1-[Top N%])
then "Bottom "+STR([Top N%]*100)+"%"
END
```

12. Drag the header field to **Columns**. The final view is as follows:

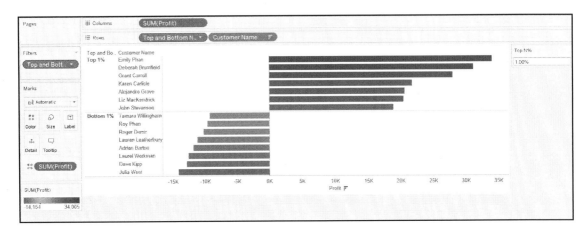

Filter without losing context

Now let's look at an example of using filter by still keeping the context you need. For example, you want to use a filter to look at customers who bought a specific type of product, but at the same time, you also want to see the other products these customers bought. I will use the Superstore data set for this example. The following steps need to be performed:

1. Drag **Customer Name** to **Rows**.
2. Drag **Product Name** to **Rows**, next to **Customer Name**.

3. I want to see all the customers who bought a certain product. For example, all the customers who bought **Printer**. If I just use **Product Name** as the filter, it will give me all the customers who bought printers, but I can't see the other products they bought.

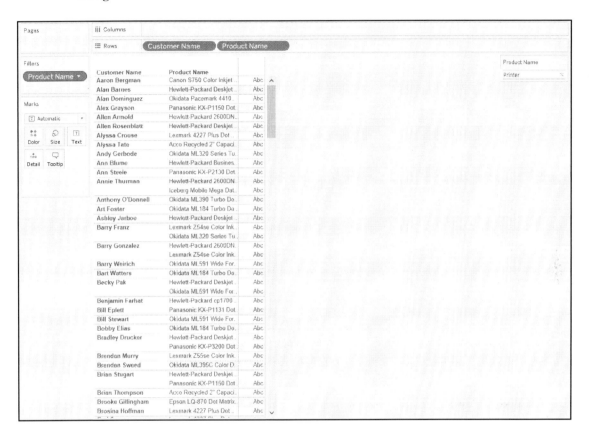

4. To be able to see all the customers who bought a certain product and all the products they bought, I need to use the filter on **calculated field**.

5. Create a parameter called `Search Product Name`.

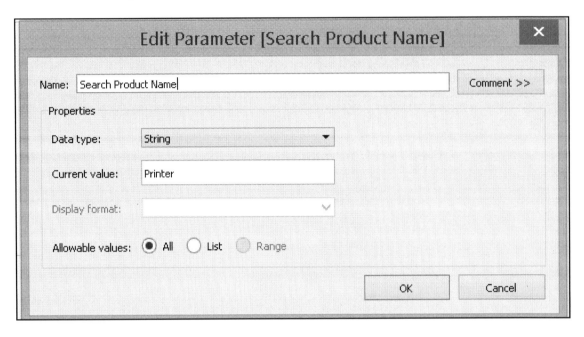

6. Create a calculated field called `Bought Product?`.

7. Create a calculated field called `Count Bought Product`.

8. Create a conditional filter on **Customer Name** using the `Count Bought Product` calculated field.

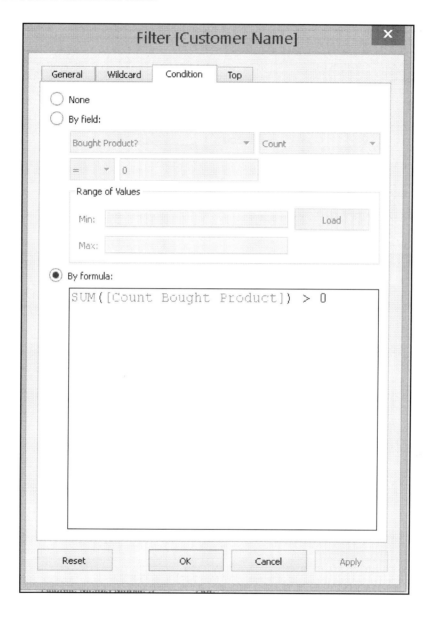

9. Now I am able to see all the customers who bought a certain product and all the products they bought.

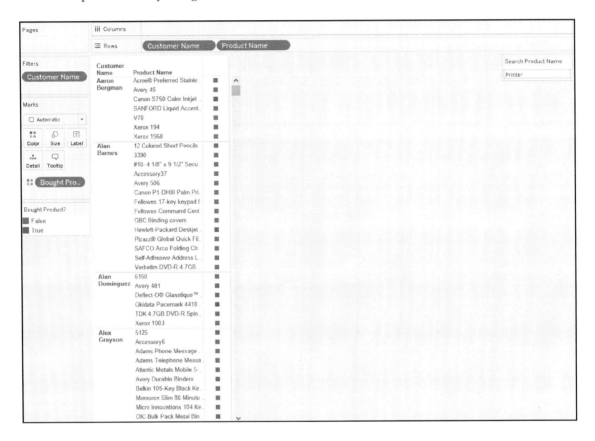

Filter with self-blending

Now let's look at an example of filtering while using self-blending. Self-blending means duplicating the data source and blending it with the original data source. I will use the Superstore data set for this example. The following steps need to be performed:

1. Drag **Product Sub-Category** to **Columns**.
2. Drag **SUM (Sales)** to **Rows**.
3. Add **Order Date** as a filter.

4. Sort **Product Sub-Category** by SUM (Sales). You will see the following:

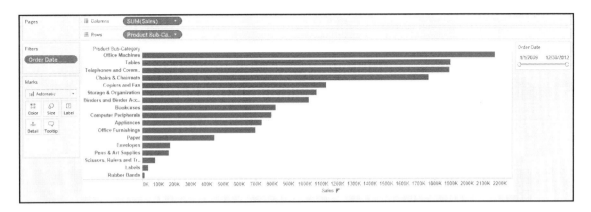

5. If I change **Order Date** to a smaller range, which is available in the data source, **SUM (Sales)** will also change to only **show the Sales** in that time range. This is the expected behavior of the **Order Date** filter.

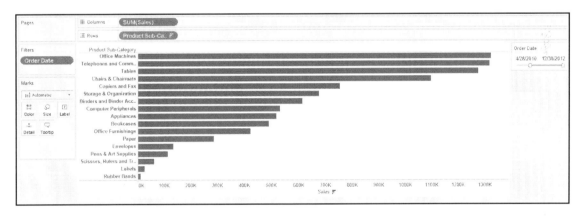

6. However, I hope I can change the **Order Year** filter to see not only the sales in a certain time period but also the whole lifetime sales for each **Product Sub-Category**. To achieve this goal, we will get some help from self-blending.

7. But before we perform self-blending, we need to do some work in the **View**. Drag **Order Date** from the original data source to **Detail mark**, and set it as **continuous**. Click on **Color mark** and change **Border color** to **None**. You will notice that when you slide the **Order Date** filter, the **SUM (Sales)** bars change, but the scale of the axis does not.

8. Duplicate the Superstore data set. Blend the duplicated data set with the original data set using **Order Date** and **Product Sub-Category**.

9. Drag **SUM (Sales)** from the duplicated data source to the **View** and set it as **dual axis**. Choose **sync axis**.
10. Change the **Marks** type to **Bar for All**.
11. Remove **Measure Values Names** from **Marks**.
12. Change the color of **Sales (SUM)** from the original data set to gray. Change the color of the **Sales (SUM)** from the duplicated data set to light gray. Change the marks of the duplicated data set to black.
13. Remove **Order Date** from **Detail mark** of the duplicated **SUM (Sales)**.
14. When you slide the **Order Date** filter, you are changing **SUM (Sales)** from the original data set, but you can still see the total **SUM (Sales)** as the light gray bar from the duplicated data set, as shown in the following figure:

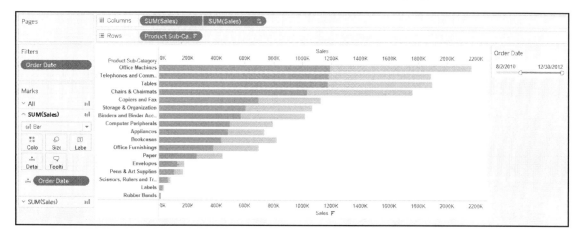

Filter, group and set

Filter, group, and set can all achieve the goal by limiting the data to be a subset of the whole data source. But they all have different use cases. The applications of filter, group, and set can be explained as follows:

- **Filter**: Filter is used to control the data shown in a view or data source to keep the minimum data needed.
- **Group**: Group is used to combine dimensions to a higher level. For example, if you are working on a data set with many sales representatives, you can create a group of those sales reps based on certain criteria such as sales territory or industry specialty or product type. Group is static once you create it. If you have new sales reps joining, you need to edit your group to assign the new sales reps to the correct group.

- **Set**: Set is used to create a data set that meets certain conditions you have defined. Any sheet within the workbook can use the set. Any workbook uses the saved data source (.tds) that has the set can also use the stored set. A set can only be created using the field in the same data set. You cannot create a set based on a field in the secondary data source.

Cascading filter

Cascading filters are filters in which the selections in the first filter can change the options in the second filter to limit them to only those values that are relevant to the first filter. This type of filter is important to prevent the user from selecting irrelevant data. It creates a better user experience. I will use the Superstore data set to walk through the example, as shown next:

1. Create **calculated field** called Territory.

```
Territory                          Orders (Sample - Superstore Sales (Excel))

IF [Region] = "Atlantic" or [Region] = "Ontario"
THEN 1
ELSEIF [Region] = "West" THEN 2
ELSE 3
END
```

2. Drag **Territory** to the **Filter** shelf, and add it to **Context**.

3. Create a parameter called `Territory Manager`, as shown in the following figure:

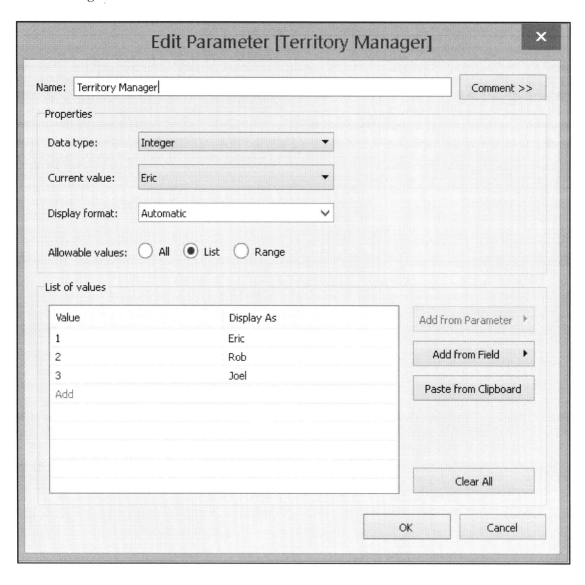

4. Create a **calculated field** called `Territory Shown`:

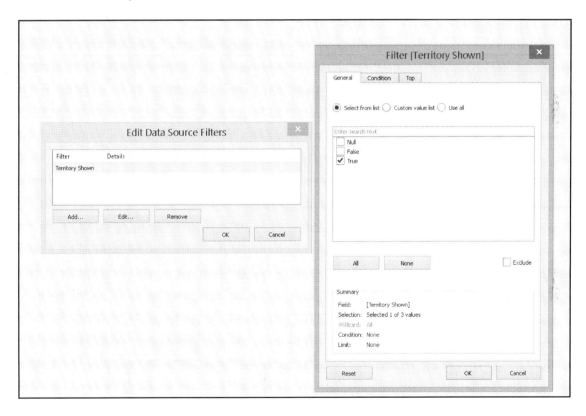

```
Territory Shown                    Orders (Sample - Superstore Sales (Excel))

[Territory] = [Territory Manager]
OR
  ([Territory] = 3 AND [Territory Manager] = 2)
OR
  ([Territory] = 2 AND [Territory Manager] = 3)|
```

5. Add **Territory Shown** to **Data Source filter**. This will be our level one filter. The **Territory Context** filter is level two, as shown next:

6. Drag **Region** to the **Filter** shelf, and add it to **Context**. This is our level three filter.

7. Create a **calculated field** called `Customer Name Filter`:

8. Drag **Customer Name Filter** to the **Filter** shelf. This is our level four filter.
9. Once you select a specific territory manager in **Territory Manager**, the other filters will show only relevant values based on your territory manager, as shown in the following figure:

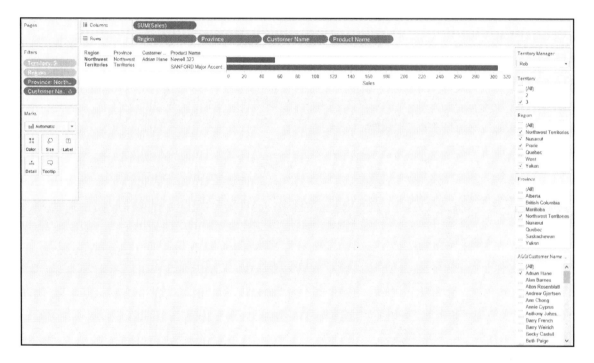

Dynamic set and filter

Dynamic set and filter means once the values in the data source change, the set or filter will automatically reflect the change of the values. It is a highly requested feature in Tableau, but it is not available yet. However, we can use some tricks to achieve this goal. In this example, I want to show the top 10 provinces by sales for certain regions. I will use the Superstore data set. The following steps need to be performed:

1. Create a set for **Province** for **Top 10 Provinces By Sales**, as shown in the following figure:

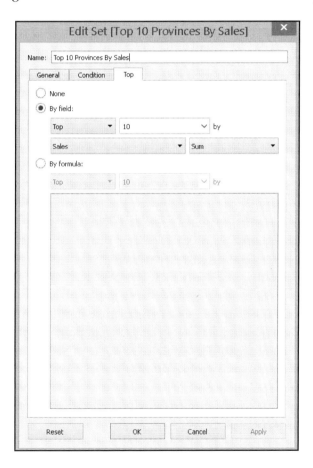

2. Create **calculated** field to use as the header for **Provinces**. If the **Province** is in the top 10 set, show Province name; otherwise, show Other:

3. Drag the header to **Columns**.
4. Drag **SUM (Sales)** to **Rows**.
5. Drag **SUM (Profit)** to the color mark. This is shown in the following figure:

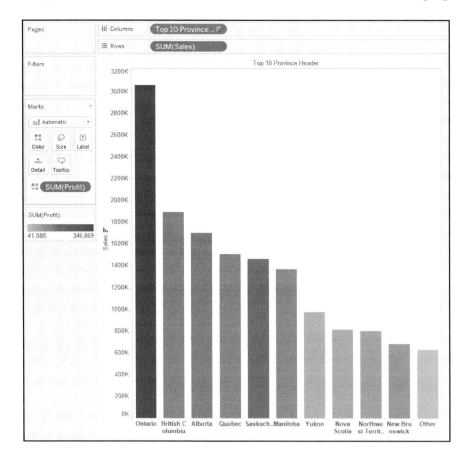

6. Now I want to add a filter for **Region**. My goal is to look at the top 10 provinces by sales for the region I selected. But if I just add the region as a filter, it will not work. This is because the set is calculated before the filter. Even if I select a certain region, the top 10 set is still calculated based on all regions. You can see in the following figure that after adding the **Region** filter, the **Top 10 Provinces** have not changed, but only the **Provinces** that are in the selected regions are shown:

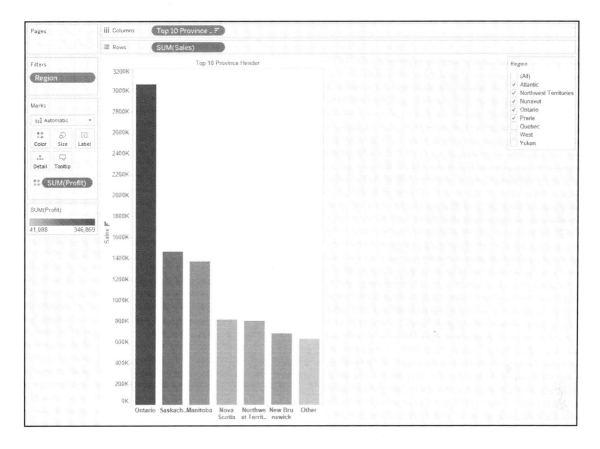

7. To solve this problem, the answer is simple. Add the **Product Category** to the context. The context filter is calculated before the set, so you will see the following view after adding the **Region** to context, which shows the **Top 10 Provinces** by sales in the selected regions, as shown next:

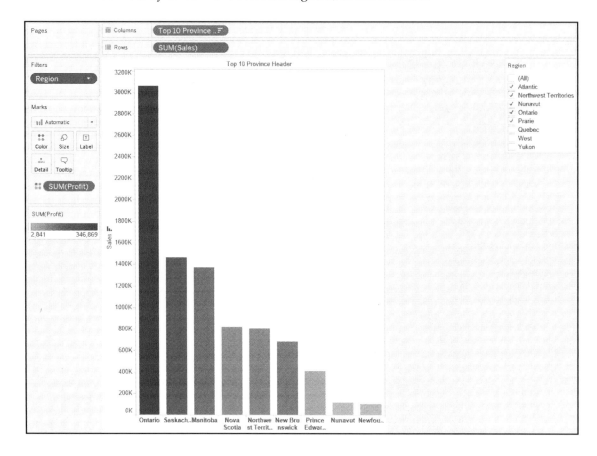

Summary

To summarize, be sure to keep in mind the following best practices for data blending: There are different types of sorting and filters. You should choose the appropriate type based on your specific use case. You should use data source filter to remove any data you do not need for your analysis.

You can use a context filter to improve efficiency and solve certain use cases, such as cascading filters. You should know the order in which Tableau executes different types of filters. Table calculations such as `Index()` and `Rank ()` are great for sorting. If you try to solve a filtering problem and do not know what to do, you can try self-blending and bring the filter/measure from the secondary data source to meet your needs. You can also filter by table calculations, such as `lookup()`. A conditional filter with a calculated field can be used to keep certain context. You should understand the differences between filter, group and set and use them based on your use case. Dynamic set and filter is highly requested but not available in Tableau now. But we can use a workaround to achieve the same goal.

In the next chapter, we will talk about how to format your visualization.

5
Formatting

In the previous chapter, we talked about how to use sort/filter to make your view more intuitive for the users to see and limit the data in the view based on your analytics needs. Now we will talk about how to format your visualization.

In this chapter, we will cover the following:

- Tooltip
- Formatting individual measure
- Date formatting
- Reference line
- Sheet selection
- Dashboard actions
- Custom color platter

Tooltip

In this section, we will discuss different ways to format a tooltip to tell amazing stories.

Custom logo in a tooltip

It is very cool to get some pictures into a tooltip to convey more compelling information. In this trick, we will learn how to add unicode icons to a tooltip.

The following table is the sales percent change year by year for each product category in `Superstore` dataset:

		Order Date		
Product Cate..	2009	2010	2011	2012
Furniture		-14.94%	1.36%	-6.78%
Office Supplies		-13.03%	-11.06%	27.18%
Technology		-17.90%	-2.17%	11.10%

It would be nice if we could use the up or down icon to show the increase or decrease in sales.

To format the sales and table calculation, click on **Calculation** and then **format**:

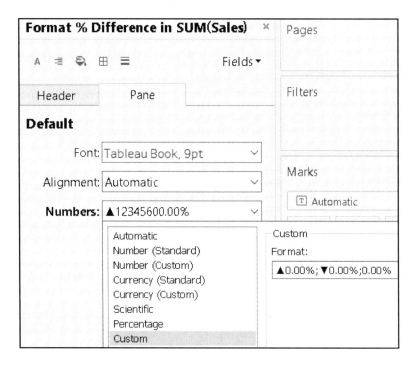

You can search for the unicode icon and copy-paste whatever you like to the **Format** box. The custom formatting in Tableau follows the format as [Positive Value]; [Negative Value]; [Zero].

The result is as follows:

Product Cate..	2009	Order Date 2010	2011	2012
Furniture		▼14.94%	▲1.36%	▼6.78%
Office Supplies		▼13.03%	▼11.06%	▲27.18%
Technology		▼17.90%	▼2.17%	▲11.10%

Now we can use the same trick to format a tooltip.

1. Create a table calculation for the percent difference in sales, as follows:

```
Sales % Difference                    Orders (Sample - Superstore Sales (Excel))

(ZN(SUM([Sales]))) - LOOKUP(ZN(SUM([Sales])), -1)) / ABS(LOOKUP(ZN(SUM([Sales])), -1))|
```

2. Create a calculated field called `PosLogo`, as shown next screenshot:

```
PosLogo                      Orders (Sample - Superstore Sales (Excel))

if [Sales % Difference]>0
then"▲"
else""
END
```

3. Create a calculated field called `NegLogo`, as follows:

```
NegLogo                      Orders (Sample - Superstore Sales (Excel))

if [Sales % Difference]<0
then "∨"
else ""
END
```

4. Add both calculations to the tooltip and change the format of **Sales % Difference**, as shown next:

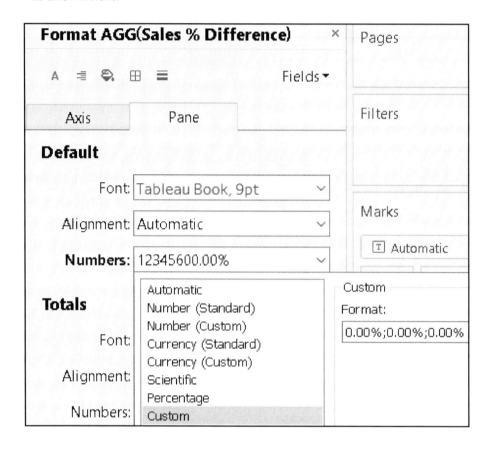

5. Edit the tooltip, as follows:

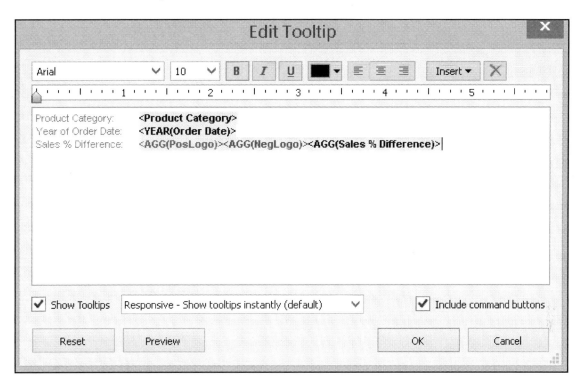

6. The result is shown next. This is when the percentage is negative; so we see a red triangle:

7. This is when the percentage is positive; so we see a green triangle:

| | Order Date | | | |
Product Category	2009	2010	2011	2012
Furniture		14.94%	1.36%	6.78%
Office Supplies		13.03%	11.06%	27.18%
Technology		17.90%	2.17%	11.10

Product Category: Office Supplies
Year of Order Date: 2012
Sales % Difference: ▲27.18%

Chart in a tooltip

Now I want to show another example of adding chart to a tooltip. I will use the Coffee Chain data set for this example.

1. First we need to create a join of the three tables in the **Coffee Chain** data set, as shown in the following figure:

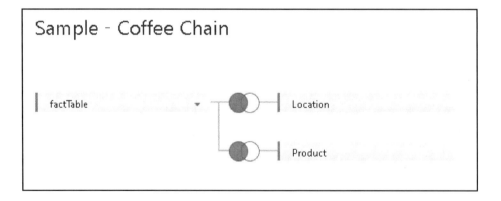

2. Then create a Viz, as shown next:

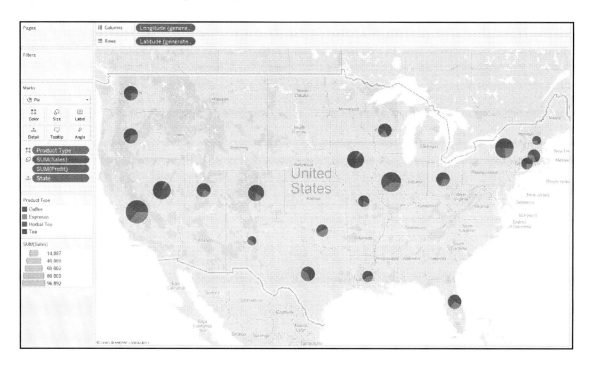

3. Edit the tooltip, as follows:

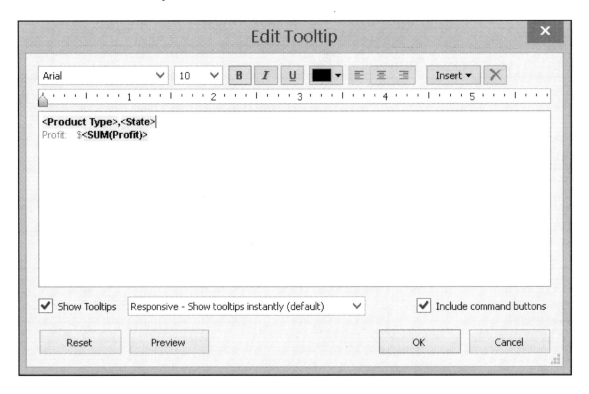

The Viz shows the **SUM (sales)** and **SUM (profit)** for each state. The tooltip shows the **SUM (Profit)**. For some states that have small sales, it is very hard to see the breakdown of sales by product type in a pie chart.

To solve this problem, I want to replace the pie chart with a bar chart that shows the percentage of sales for each product type in each state. First let's create the bar chart in a new worksheet. Then we will add the bar chart to the tooltip.

1. To create the bar chart that shows the percent of sales by product type in each state, create the following calculated fields for each of the four product types.

2. The following is the calculation for coffee:

```
% Sales Coffee                    Sample - Coffee Chain

(SUM(IIF([Product Type]="Coffee",[Sales],0))/SUM([Sales]))*100
```

3. The calculation for espresso is as follows:

```
% Sales Espresso                    Sample - Coffee Chain

(SUM(IIF([Product Type]="Espresso",[Sales],0))/SUM([Sales]))*100
```

4. The calculation for herbal tea is shown next:

```
% Sales Herbal Tea                  Sample - Coffee Chain

(SUM(IIF([Product Type]="Herbal Tea",[Sales],0))/SUM([Sales]))*100
```

5. The following shows the calculation for tea:

```
% Sales Tea                         Sample - Coffee Chain

(SUM(IIF([Product Type]="Tea",[Sales],0))/SUM([Sales]))*100
```

6. Create a parameter as the `Bar`:

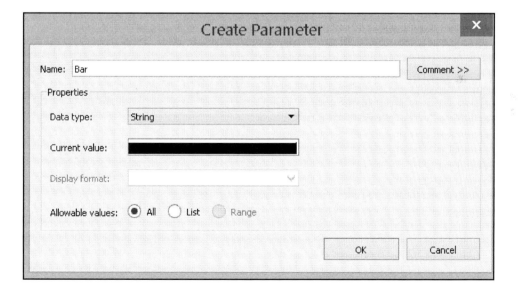

The bar is composed 100 *Alt+219* ASCII character.

Then we create the following calculated fields to make the size of the bar based on the percent of sales.

1. Here is the calculation for coffee:

2. Look at the following calculation for espresso:

3. The calculation for herbal tea is as follows:

4. The following is the calculation for tea:

5. Use the calculated fields to create a **Viz**, as shown next:

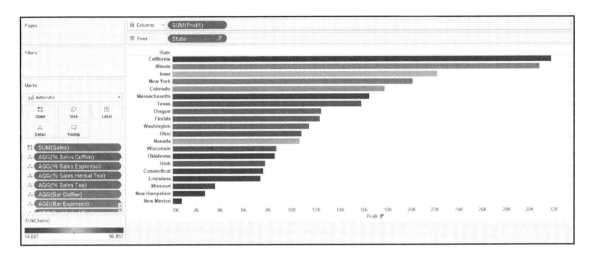

6. Duplicate the worksheet we just created, and choose **Show Me** as **map**.
7. Edit the tooltip, as follows:

8. Now we can see even for those states that have small sales, we can see the breakdown of sales by product type clearly:

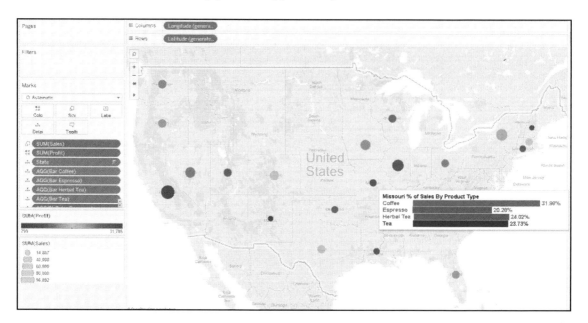

Formatting individual measure

In the previous section, we talked about how to format a tooltip. In this section, we will walk through how to format individual measure in Tableau. It is very similar to the conditional formatting in Excel.

Colour code individual measure

Most of us are familiar with the conditional-formatting feature in Excel, which allows you to format individual cells based on certain rules. However, it is not a built-in feature for Tableau to format individual measure. If you have multiple measures in the **View**, you have to follow the same rules as you have on the **Mark** shelf. But we will learn a trick that can allow us to format individual measure. The trick is to create a fake header for each measure that you want to format so you can get a separate **Mark** for each measure.

For example, in the **Orders** table of Superstore data set, when you have multiple measures in the **View**, you are likely to have them in the **Measure Names** on **Rows** and **Measure Values** in **Text**, as shown in the following figure:

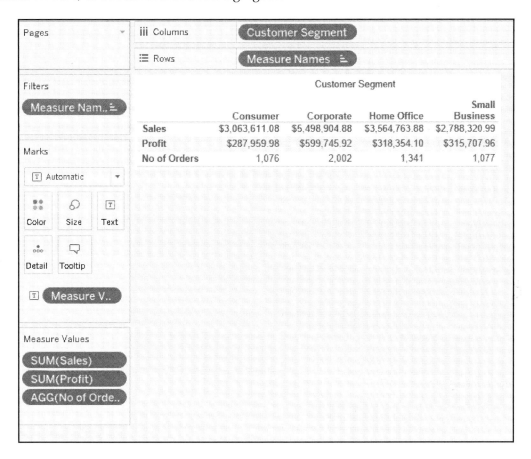

If you want to color code the measure, you can create a rule using a calculated field and drag that calculated field to the **Color** shelf. Now I will create a calculated field to see whether my profit reaches the goal or not, as follows:

When I drag the **Profit Goal** to the **Color** shelf, my View looks as shown next:

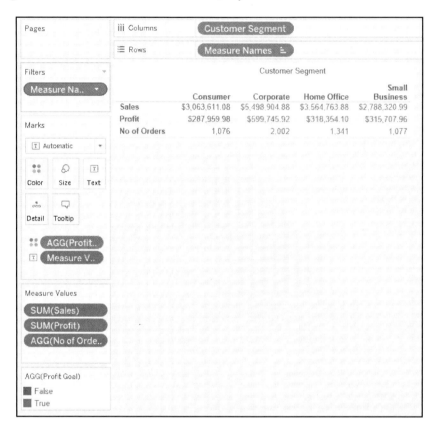

You will see that all the measures in the View are color coded based on the **Profit Goal**, which does not make sense since I may have different rules for other measures.

To solve this problem, let's create a fake header for each measure so they can each have a separate **Mark**.

1. Create a calculated field, as follows:

2. Create a calculated field, as shown next. This field is used to separate the values in the **Customer Segment** to avoid overlapping text:

3. Build a view, as follows:

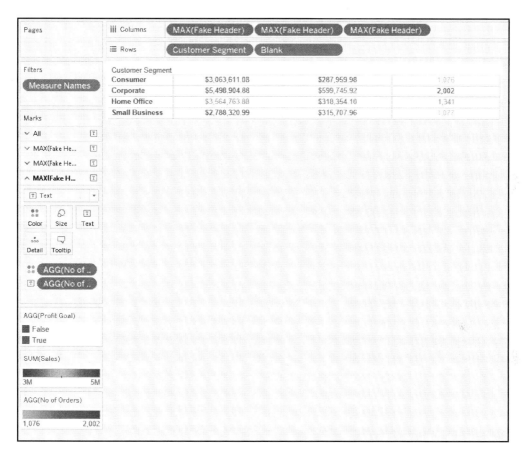

Since each measure in the view has a separate **Mark**, we can format them differently.

Fill cell with different color

You may say that we are only color coding the values in the cells but not changing the filled color of the cell. There is another trick to do that.

Following the aforementioned example, let's add a fake header to the mark for sales and change the mark type from **Text** to **Gantt Bar**, as shown in the following figure:

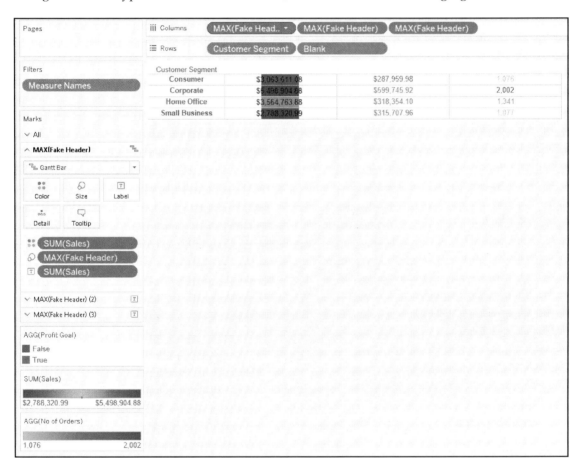

You will notice that the **Gantt Bar** does not fill the entire cell. The trick to solve this issue is to show the header of the fake header on **Columns** and edit the **Axis**, as follows:

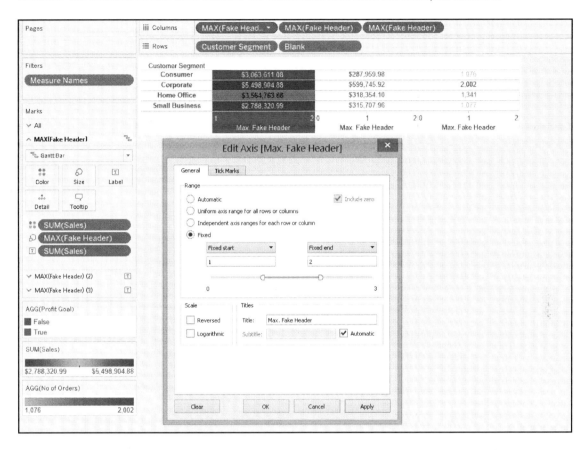

Hide the header again, and you will see the cells are filled with different colors:

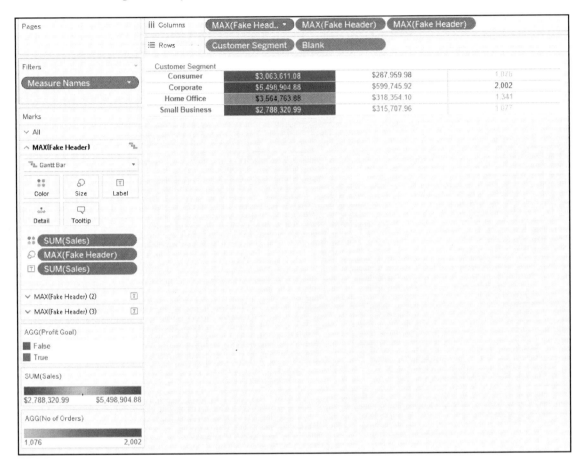

Date formatting

In the previous section, we talked about how to format individual measure. In this section, we will discuss how to format date.

Time range

If you know that the duration of your time range will be always less than 24 hours, you can use the built-in format of time range. If your time range is not in seconds, you need to change it to seconds and then start formatting. It is very simple to get the time range into seconds using `DATEDIFF ('second',[Order Date],[Ship Date])`.

After changing the time range to seconds, you can create another calculated field as `DATETIME ([Time Range (seconds)]/86400)`. Then set the format of this calculated field as custom *hh:mm:ss* (note that the lower case mm is minutes and the upper case MM is month), as shown next:

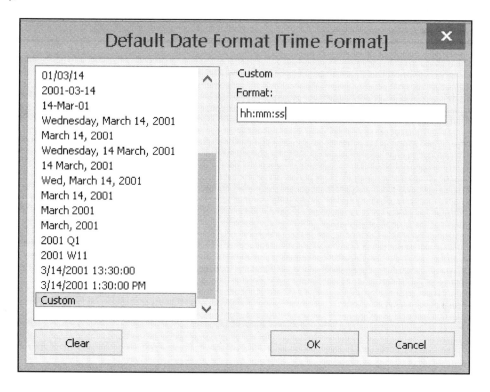

Since the **Order Date** and **Ship Date** in the Superstore data set is at day level, in order to get some time range that is less than 24 hours, I changed my calculation to `DATEDIFF('second',[Order Date],[Ship Date])-86000`. The result is as follows:

Row ID	Order ID	Time Range (seconds)	Time Format	Order Date	Ship Date
1	3	518800	00:06:40	10/13/2010	10/20/2010
2	6	400	00:06:40	2/20/2012	2/21/2012
3	32	86800	00:06:40	7/15/2011	7/17/2011
4	32	400	00:06:40	7/15/2011	7/16/2011
5	32	86800	00:06:40	7/15/2011	7/17/2011
6	32	400	00:06:40	7/15/2011	7/16/2011
7	35	400	00:06:40	10/22/2011	10/23/2011
8	35	86800	00:06:40	10/22/2011	10/24/2011
9	36	-86000	00:06:40	11/2/2011	11/2/2011
10	65	400	00:06:40	3/17/2011	3/18/2011
11	66	-86000	00:06:40	1/19/2009	1/19/2009
12	69	86800	00:06:40	6/3/2009	6/5/2009
13	69	86800	00:06:40	6/3/2009	6/5/2009
14	70	346000	00:06:40	12/17/2010	12/22/2010
15	70	346000	00:06:40	12/17/2010	12/22/2010
16	96	86800	00:06:40	4/16/2009	4/18/2009
17	97	400	00:06:40	1/28/2010	1/29/2010
18	129	691600	00:06:40	11/18/2012	11/27/2012
19	130	86800	00:06:40	5/7/2012	5/9/2012
20	130	400	00:06:40	5/7/2012	5/8/2012
21	130	173200	00:06:40	5/7/2012	5/10/2012
22	132	400	00:06:40	6/10/2010	6/11/2010
23	132	173200	00:06:40	6/10/2010	6/13/2010
24	134	86800	00:06:40	4/30/2012	5/2/2012
25	135	86800	00:06:40	10/20/2011	10/22/2011
26	166	86800	00:06:40	9/11/2011	9/13/2011

You can see that the result is accurate for **400** seconds but wrong for **86800** seconds.

How do we solve this issue? We can create a calculated field using percent:

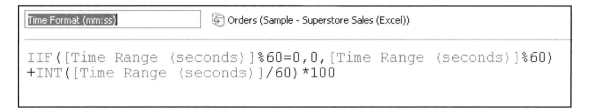

The first line of this calculation is using percent to get the seconds, the second line is to get the minutes. Set the format of the calculated field as custom `00:00`:

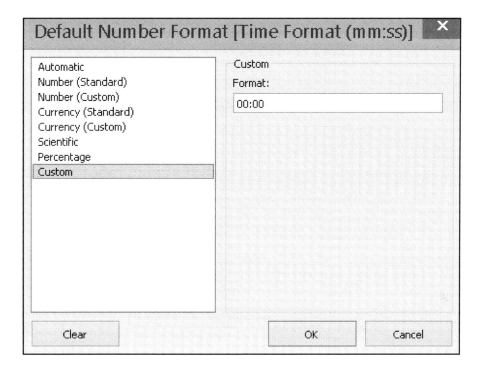

The result is as follows:

Row ID	Order ID	Time Format (mm:ss)	Time Range (seconds)	Time Format	Order Date	Ship Date
1	3	8646:40	518800	00:06:40	10/13/2010	10/20/2010
2	6	06:40	400	00:06:40	2/20/2012	2/21/2012
3	32	1446:40	86800	00:06:40	7/15/2011	7/17/2011
4	32	06:40	400	00:06:40	7/15/2011	7/16/2011
5	32	1446:40	86800	00:06:40	7/15/2011	7/17/2011
6	32	06:40	400	00:06:40	7/15/2011	7/16/2011
7	35	06:40	400	00:06:40	10/22/2011	10/23/2011
8	35	1446:40	86800	00:06:40	10/22/2011	10/24/2011
9	36	-1433:20	-86000	00:06:40	11/2/2011	11/2/2011
10	65	06:40	400	00:06:40	3/17/2011	3/18/2011
11	66	-1433:20	-86000	00:06:40	1/19/2009	1/19/2009
12	69	1446:40	86800	00:06:40	6/3/2009	6/5/2009
13	69	1446:40	86800	00:06:40	6/3/2009	6/5/2009
14	70	5766:40	346000	00:06:40	12/17/2010	12/22/2010
15	70	5766:40	346000	00:06:40	12/17/2010	12/22/2010
16	96	1446:40	86800	00:06:40	4/16/2009	4/18/2009
17	97	06:40	400	00:06:40	1/28/2010	1/29/2010
18	129	11526:40	691600	00:06:40	11/18/2012	11/27/2012
19	130	1446:40	86800	00:06:40	5/7/2012	5/9/2012
20	130	06:40	400	00:06:40	5/7/2012	5/8/2012
21	130	2886:40	173200	00:06:40	5/7/2012	5/10/2012
22	132	06:40	400	00:06:40	6/10/2010	6/11/2010
23	132	2886:40	173200	00:06:40	6/10/2010	6/13/2010
24	134	1446:40	86800	00:06:40	4/30/2012	5/2/2012
25	135	1446:40	86800	00:06:40	10/20/2011	10/22/2011
26	166	1446:40	86800	00:06:40	9/11/2011	9/13/2011

You will see now that the result for **86800** is accurate.

But this still does not look good. We want to be able to show *hh:mm:ss*. It is as simple as adding one more line to the previous calculation:

Time Format (hh:mm:ss)		Orders (Sample - Superstore Sales (Excel))

```
IIF([Time Range (seconds)] % 60 =0,0,[Time Range (seconds)] % 60)
+ IIF(INT([Time Range (seconds)]/60) %60 =0, 0, INT([Time Range (seconds)]/60) %60) * 100
+ INT([Time Range (seconds)]/3600) * 10000
```

The first line of this calculation is using % to get the seconds, the second line is to get the minutes, and the third line is to calculate the hours. Set the format of the **calculated field** as **Custom 00:00:00**. The result is as follows:

Row ID	Order ID	Time Format (hh:mm:ss)	Time Format (mm:ss)	Time Range (seconds)	Time Format	Order Date	Ship Date	
1	3	144:06:40	8646:40	518800	00:06:40	10/13/2010	10/20/2010	Abc
2	6	00:06:40	06:40	400	00:06:40	2/20/2012	2/21/2012	Abc
3	32	24:06:40	1446:40	86800	00:06:40	7/15/2011	7/17/2011	Abc
4	32	00:06:40	06:40	400	00:06:40	7/15/2011	7/16/2011	Abc
5	32	24:06:40	1446:40	86800	00:06:40	7/15/2011	7/17/2011	Abc
6	32	00:06:40	06:40	400	00:06:40	7/15/2011	7/16/2011	Abc
7	35	00:06:40	06:40	400	00:06:40	10/22/2011	10/23/2011	Abc
8	35	24:06:40	1446:40	86800	00:06:40	10/22/2011	10/24/2011	Abc
9	36	-23:53:20	-1433:20	-86000	00:06:40	11/2/2011	11/2/2011	Abc
10	65	00:06:40	06:40	400	00:06:40	3/17/2011	3/18/2011	Abc
11	66	-23:53:20	-1433:20	-86000	00:06:40	1/19/2009	1/19/2009	Abc
12	69	24:06:40	1446:40	86800	00:06:40	6/3/2009	6/5/2009	Abc
13	69	24:06:40	1446:40	86800	00:06:40	6/3/2009	6/5/2009	Abc
14	70	96:06:40	5766:40	346000	00:06:40	12/17/2010	12/22/2010	Abc
15	70	96:06:40	5766:40	346000	00:06:40	12/17/2010	12/22/2010	Abc
16	96	24:06:40	1446:40	86800	00:06:40	4/16/2009	4/18/2009	Abc
17	97	00:06:40	06:40	400	00:06:40	1/28/2010	1/29/2010	Abc
18	129	192:06:40	11526:40	691600	00:06:40	11/18/2012	11/27/2012	Abc
19	130	24:06:40	1446:40	86800	00:06:40	5/7/2012	5/9/2012	Abc
20	130	00:06:40	06:40	400	00:06:40	5/7/2012	5/8/2012	Abc
21	130	48:06:40	2886:40	173200	00:06:40	5/7/2012	5/10/2012	Abc
22	132	00:06:40	06:40	400	00:06:40	6/10/2010	6/11/2010	Abc
23	132	48:06:40	2886:40	173200	00:06:40	6/10/2010	6/13/2010	Abc
24	134	24:06:40	1446:40	86800	00:06:40	4/30/2012	5/2/2012	Abc
25	135	24:06:40	1446:40	86800	00:06:40	10/20/2011	10/22/2011	Abc
26	166	24:06:40	1446:40	86800	00:06:40	9/11/2011	9/13/2011	Abc

The last challenge is to make it dd:hh:mm:ss. This is done using the same logic:

```
Time Format (dd:hh:mm:ss)          Orders (Sample - Superstore Sales (Excel))

IIF([Time Range (seconds)] % 60 =0,0,[Time Range (seconds)] % 60)
+ IIF(INT([Time Range (seconds)]/60) %60 =0, 0, INT([Time Range (seconds)]/60) %60) * 100
+ IIF(INT([Time Range (seconds)]/3600) %24 =0, 0, INT([Time Range (seconds)]/3600) %24) * 10000
+ INT([Time Range (seconds)]/86400) * 1000000
```

The first line of this calculation is using % to get the seconds, the second line is to get the minutes, the third line is to calculate the hours, and the fourth line is to calculate the days. Set the format of the calculated field as custom *00:00:00:00*. The result is as follows:

Row ID	Order ID	Time Format (dd: hh:mm:ss)	Time Format (hh:mm:ss)	Time Format (mm:ss)	Time Range (seconds)	Time Format	Order Date	Ship Date
1	3	06:00:06:40	144:06:40	8646:40	518800	00:06:40	10/13/2010	10/20/2010
2	6	00:00:06:40	00:06:40	06:40	400	00:06:40	2/20/2012	2/21/2012
3	32	01:00:06:40	24:06:40	1446:40	86800	00:06:40	7/15/2011	7/17/2011
4	32	00:00:06:40	00:06:40	06:40	400	00:06:40	7/15/2011	7/16/2011
5	32	01:00:06:40	24:06:40	1446:40	86800	00:06:40	7/15/2011	7/17/2011
6	32	00:00:06:40	00:06:40	06:40	400	00:06:40	7/15/2011	7/16/2011
7	35	00:00:06:40	00:06:40	06:40	400	00:06:40	10/22/2011	10/23/2011
8	35	01:00:06:40	24:06:40	1446:40	86800	00:06:40	10/22/2011	10/24/2011
9	36	-00:23:53:20	-23:53:20	-1433:20	-86000	00:06:40	11/2/2011	11/2/2011
10	65	00:00:06:40	00:06:40	06:40	400	00:06:40	3/17/2011	3/18/2011
11	66	-00:23:53:20	-23:53:20	-1433:20	-86000	00:06:40	1/19/2009	1/19/2009
12	69	01:00:06:40	24:06:40	1446:40	86800	00:06:40	6/3/2009	6/5/2009
13	69	01:00:06:40	24:06:40	1446:40	86800	00:06:40	6/3/2009	6/5/2009
14	70	04:00:06:40	96:06:40	5766:40	346000	00:06:40	12/17/2010	12/22/2010
15	70	04:00:06:40	96:06:40	5766:40	346000	00:06:40	12/17/2010	12/22/2010
16	96	01:00:06:40	24:06:40	1446:40	86800	00:06:40	4/16/2009	4/18/2009
17	97	00:00:06:40	00:06:40	06:40	400	00:06:40	1/28/2010	1/29/2010
18	129	08:00:06:40	192:06:40	11526:40	691600	00:06:40	11/18/2012	11/27/2012
19	130	01:00:06:40	24:06:40	1446:40	86800	00:06:40	5/7/2012	5/9/2012
20	130	00:00:06:40	00:06:40	06:40	400	00:06:40	5/7/2012	5/8/2012
21	130	02:00:06:40	48:06:40	2886:40	173200	00:06:40	5/7/2012	5/10/2012
22	132	00:00:06:40	00:06:40	06:40	400	00:06:40	6/10/2010	6/11/2010
23	132	02:00:06:40	48:06:40	2886:40	173200	00:06:40	6/10/2010	6/13/2010
24	134	01:00:06:40	24:06:40	1446:40	86800	00:06:40	4/30/2012	5/2/2012
25	135	01:00:06:40	24:06:40	1446:40	86800	00:06:40	10/20/2011	10/22/2011
26	166	01:00:06:40	24:06:40	1446:40	86800	00:06:40	9/11/2011	9/13/2011

Though it seems like this solution is very good, there is an issue when calculating the SUM of the time range. If you are using a SUM function or the Grand Total, the time range will not add up correctly. The issue is related to the Tableau's order of operation. The SUM or Grand Total are not calculated when the formatting is done. Tableau first gets the data from the data source and then computes all the calculations (including the formatting calculation), then aggregates the calculations to Sum or Grand Total. The last step is formatting the view. The formatting calculation should happen after the SUM or Grand Total is calculated based on the raw time range in seconds. However, it is actually done after the formatting calculation is done. For example, you are adding *100* seconds to *100* seconds. The *SUM (100,100) = 100 + 100 = 200 seconds = 03:20*. However, Tableau is doing *100 + 100 = 01:40 + 01:40 = 02:80*.

The solution to this issue is to do the aggregation before the format calculation. We can simply replace the **Time Range (seconds)** with **SUM (Time Range (seconds))**. The new calculation is as follows:

```
Time Format (mm:ss) (SUM)                    Orders (Sample - Superstore Sales (Excel))

IIF(SUM([Time Range (seconds)])%60=0,0,SUM([Time Range (seconds)])%60)
+INT(SUM([Time Range (seconds)])/60)*100
```

Reference line

Tableau allows you to add reference line to your visualization. For example, if you are analyzing the monthly sales, you can add a reference line for average sales so you can see how each month is performing against the average. In the previous section, we learned about formatting date. In this section, we will talk about how to create different types of reference lines.

Reference line with 45 degree

Sometimes we want to build a scatter plot and analyze the relationship between the x and y axes. It will be nice if we have a 45 degree reference line in the scatter plot so we can easily see which axis is bigger.

For example, I want to compare the percent of consumer sales and the percent of corporate sales in the superstore data set.

1. First I will create two calculated fields to get the percent sales of consumer and corporate customers.
2. This is the calculation for Consumer Sales:

%Consumer Sales	Orders (Sample - Superstore Sales (Excel))

```
(SUM(IIF([Customer Segment]="Consumer",[Sales],0))/SUM([Sales]))
```

3. This is the calculation for Corporate Sales:

%Corporate Sales	Orders (Sample - Superstore Sales (Excel))

```
(SUM(IIF([Customer Segment]="Corporate",[Sales],0))/SUM([Sales]))
```

4. Then create a view, as follows:

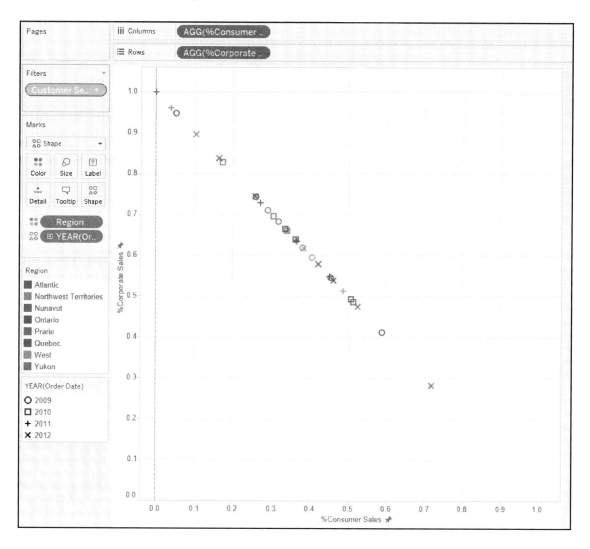

5. Note that I add the following filter and add it as context filter because I want to analyze only the percent of sales for consumer and corporate customers and exclude other customer segments. This is shown next:

6. Now create a calculated field for the reference line:

7. Add the reference line calculated field to the view and choose **Dual axis**.

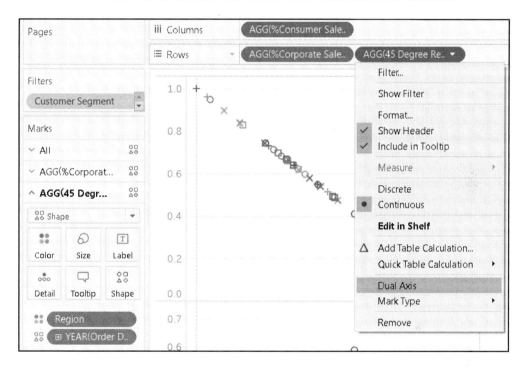

8. Right click the 45 degree reference line axis and choose **Synchronize axis**:

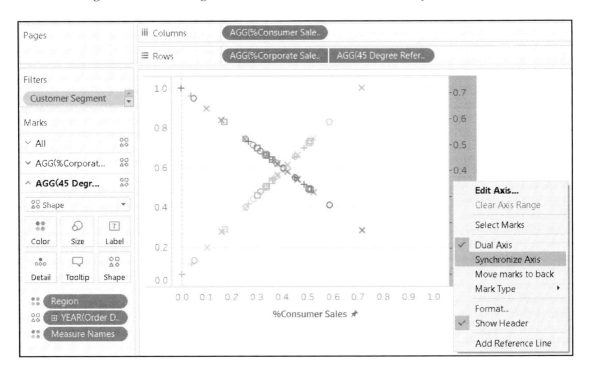

9. Edit the mark of the 45 degree reference line, as follows:

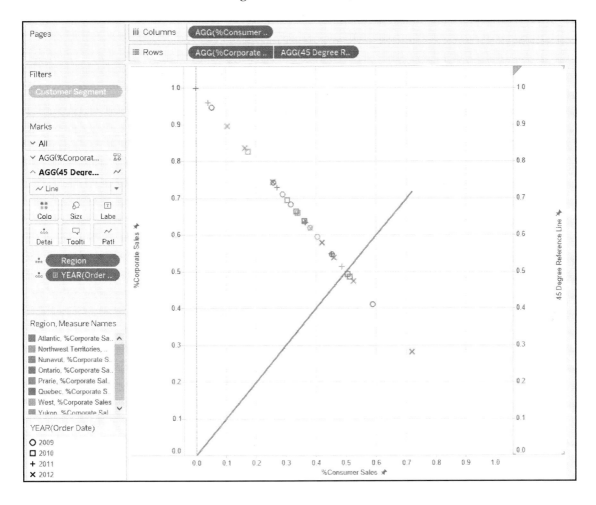

10. Edit the tooltip, as follows:

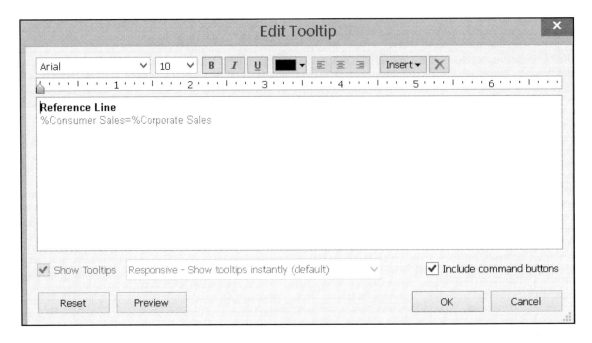

11. Uncheck the **Show header** of the 45 degree reference line on **Rows**. The final view is as follows:

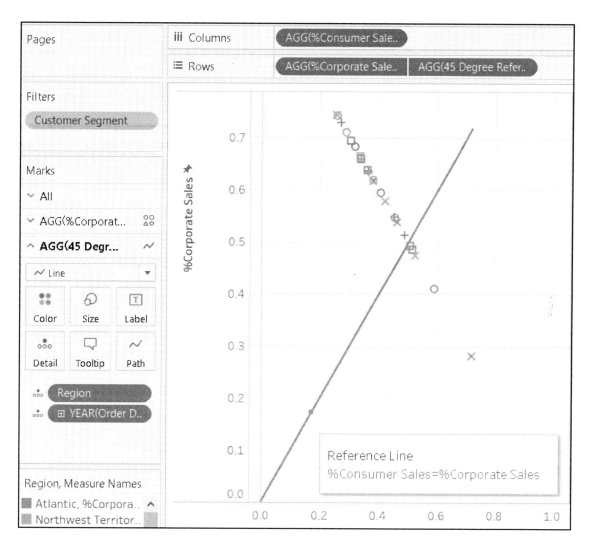

Sheet selection

Now we will learn the trick about how to create a sheet selector to show all or certain worksheets in the dashboard.

For example, I have the following dashboard with three worksheets:

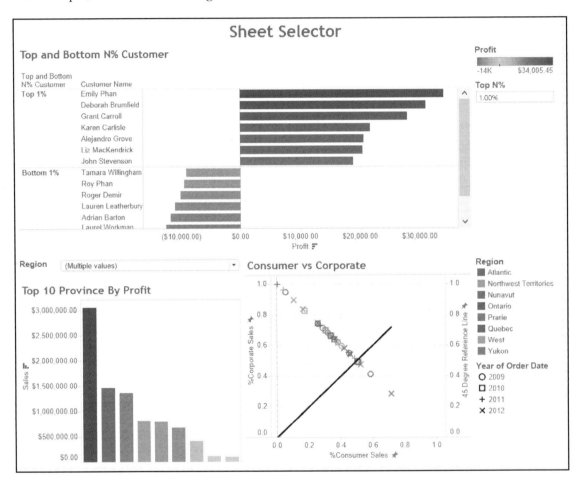

1. Create a parameter as follows:

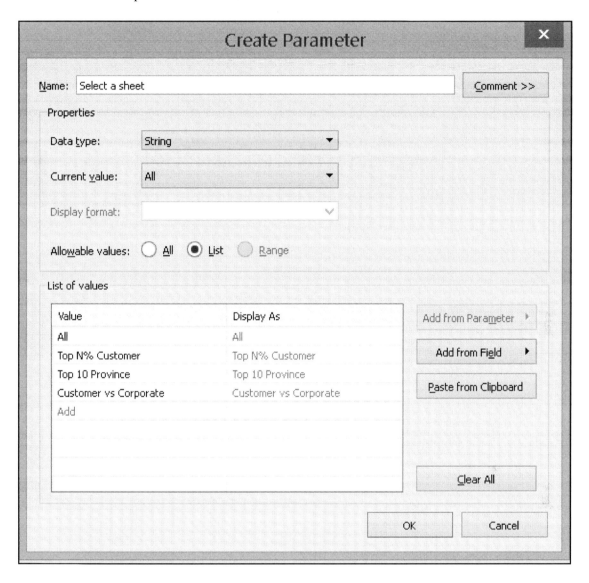

2. Create a calculated field as follows:

3. For each of the worksheets in the dashboard, add **Sheet Display** calculated field to filter and edit the filter, as follows:

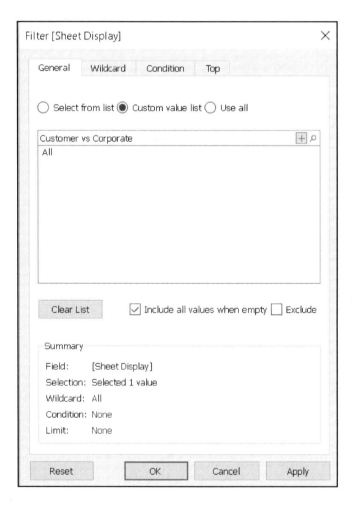

4. Create a new dashboard, add a vertical layout container to it. Then add all the worksheets to the dashboard. Hide the titles for the worksheets. Add **Select a sheet parameter** to the dashboard.

5. Now you can use the **Select a sheet parameter** to choose the specific worksheets you want to display.

6. If you choose to display `All` sheets, you can see all sheets in the dashboard:

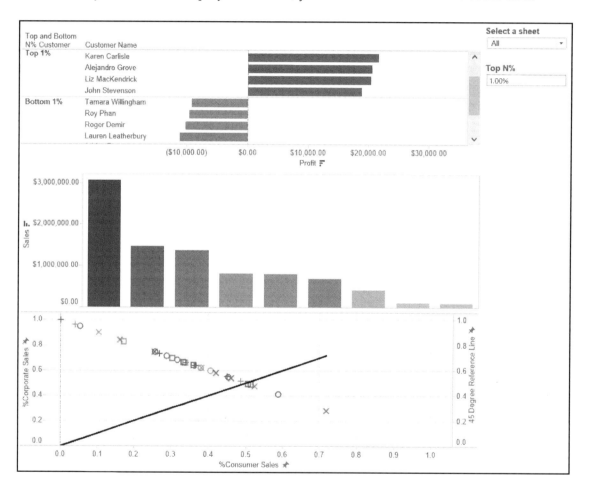

7. If you choose to display `Top N% Customer sheet`, you can see only that sheet in the dashboard:

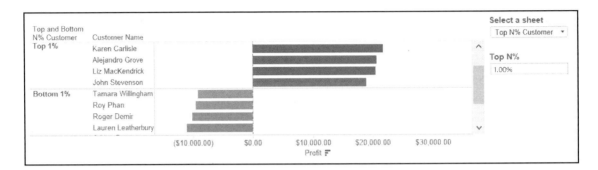

Dashboard actions

In the previous section, we learned how to build a sheet selection tool for our dashboard. In this section, we will talk about different use cases of dashboard action. Tableau allows you to interactivity to your dashboard using dashboard action. You can add link to a website, file and other Tableau worksheets to your dashboard. It also allows you to filter the data in one worksheet based the data in another. Now let's deep five into some useful use cases of dashboard action.

Action on blended field

Now, let's learn a trick about dashboard action on blended field.

1. Created a calculated filed in Superstore dataset as follows:

```
Region Type                    Orders (Sample - Superstore Sales (Excel))

IF [Region] = "Quebec"
THEN  "East"
ELSEIF [Region] = "West" THEN "West"
elseif  [Region] = "Ontario" then "South"
ELSE  "Central"
END
```

2. Blend the **Coffee Chain** data set with Superstore as shown in the next image:

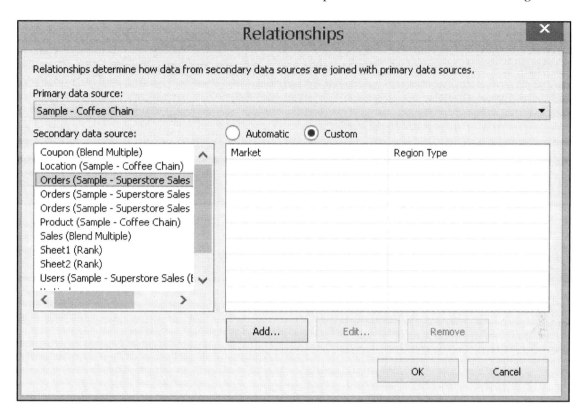

3. Create a worksheet with the Coffee Chain data set as follows:

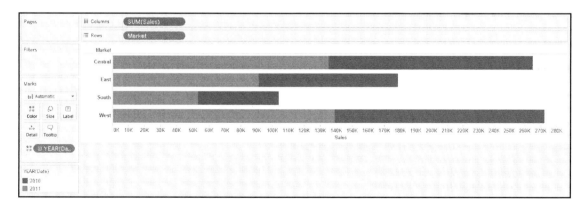

4. Create a worksheet with the Superstore data set as follows:

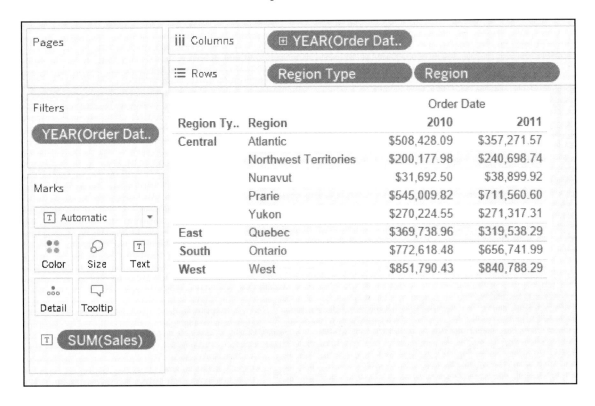

5. Create a dashboard as shown in the next image:

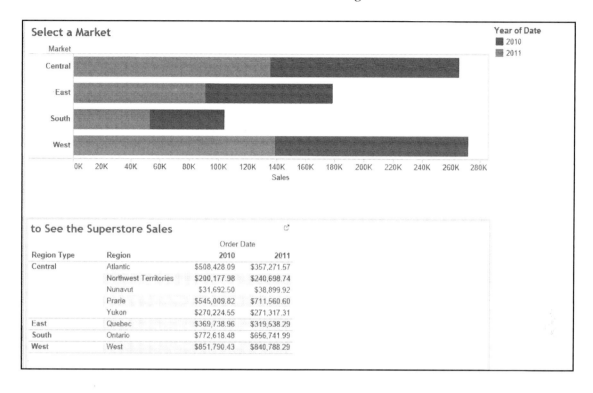

6. Set up the dashboard action, as follows. The important thing is that since you are taking action on the blended field, you need to choose **Selected Fields** and specify the **Source Field** and **Target Field/Target Data Source**. Otherwise, the action will not work. Take a look at the following figure:

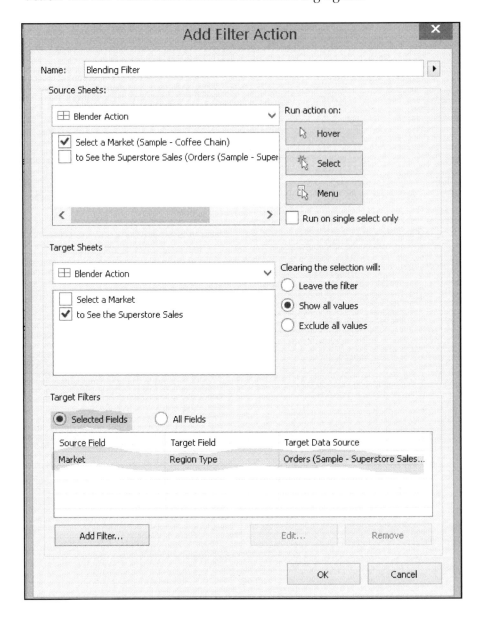

7. Now if you select a **Market** in Coffee Chain, you will see the sales of Superstore in the selected regions:

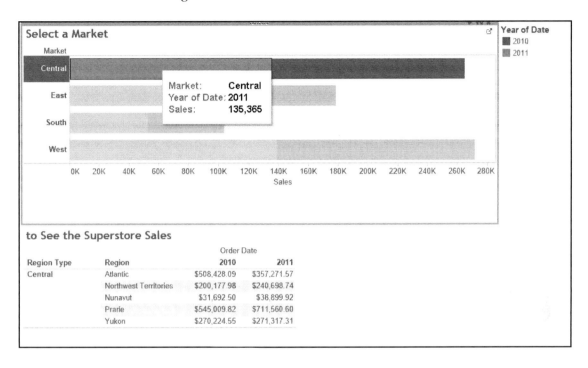

Exclude filter action

Assume that you have a dashboard as shown next, which has a tree map that shows the sales by product category/region, and a table with more details, such as **Customer Name** and **Product Name**. Most of the time, we will use the tree map as a filter so when you select a specific product category/region, you can see the details in the table. This is shown as follows:

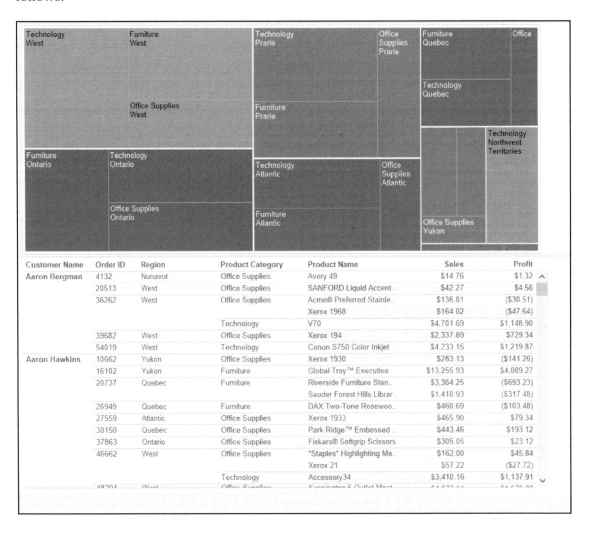

However, if the detail table is huge, it might be better to hide the table initially since a big table can take a long time to load. And then when someone selects certain product type/region, the table will show details based on the selection.

Now let's look at how to do this.

1. Add a filter dashboard action, as shown next:

2. After adding the filter action, nothing will happen initially. But if you click on one of the **product categories/regions** in the tree map and unselect it, the detail table will disappear.

3. It is better to add some instructions to the dashboard, as follows:

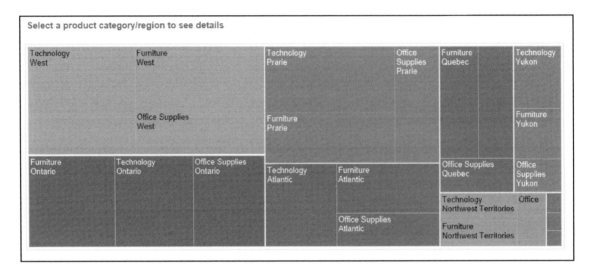

4. After selecting a **product category/region**, you can see the details in the detail table:

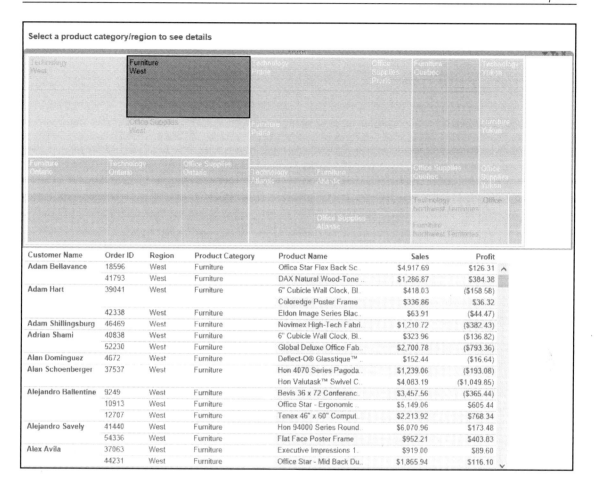

Tips for color blind

It is important to keep in mind some rules for colorblind when creating visualizations. I want to specifically talk about red and green since that is one of the most common color blind scenarios.

The trick to resolve colorblind in red and green is to reduce the saturation of the green color.

Color is either represented in **RGB** (**red, green, blue**) or **HSL** (**hue, saturation, luminance**). Since most of us are familiar with RGB, I would like to explain more of HSL:

- Hue is the color itself
- Saturation is how deep the color is-Adding white can reduce saturation.
- Luminance is how bright the color is-Adding grey can reduce luminance.

For the red-green color-blind people, the red and green look the same. But if you reduce the saturation of the green, it looks different from the red that has the regular saturation.

It is better to reduce the saturation of green because we normally want to highlight the red. The color with the higher saturation will catch people's attention more easily.

So now you may wonder how we set it up in Tableau. There are a few ways to do it.

If you need to use only red and green, you can use the traffic light color palette. The default Tableau color palette has all the colors with the same saturation. In the traffic light palette, there is the regular green and also a green with lower saturation.

Summary

To summarize, you should keep in mind the following best practices for data blending. You can customize your tooltips to tell a better story. You can add chart to tooltip if needed. You can use a fake header to color code individual measure. You can custom formatting for date duration. You can create sheet selector to show certain sheets in dashboard. You can use dashboard action to filter content in dashboard. When building visualizations, you should keep in mind some color blind tips.

In the next chapter, we will talk about how to create different types of visualizations.

6
Visualization

In the previous chapter, we talked about how to format your visualization. In this chapter, we will talk about how to create different types of visualizations, mainly focusing on creating different types of dashboards.

In this chapter, we will cover the following:

- Custom shape
- Bar and line charts
- Tree map bar chart
- Stacked bar chart
- Scatterplot
- Waffle chart
- Jitter chart
- Circle chart
- Network graph
- Calendar heat map
- Multiple small maps
- Cohort analysis
- Visualize survey data

Custom shape

Sometimes you may want to add custom shapes to your Tableau Viz. For example, the following Viz in Tableau public has used custom shapes to visualize 773 Pokemon characters:

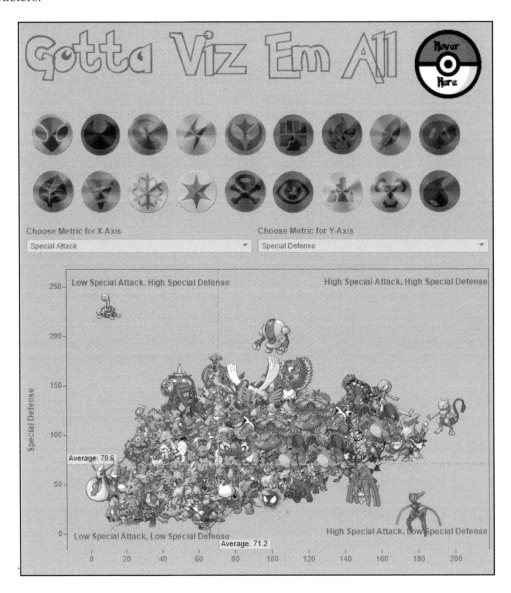

It is actually very simple to add custom shapes in Tableau; the following steps need to be performed:

1. Save your shape images as `.jpeg`, `.png`, `.bmp`, or `.gif`.

2. Copy the images to a folder in `My Tableau Repository | Shapes`. You can name the folder anything you like, and the folder name will be the shape palette name in Tableau. As an example, I created this folder called **Emoji**, as shown next:

3. In Tableau, click on the **Shape** mark and choose **More Shapes**:

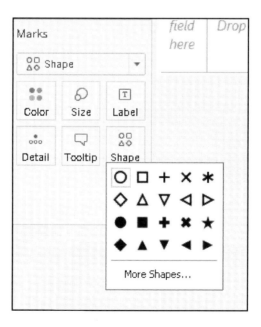

4. Click on **Reload Shapes**; you will see the Emoji shape palette in the dropdown list:

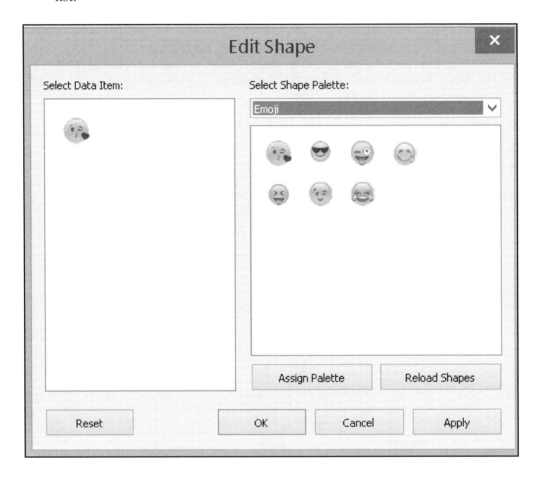

Bar and line charts

Tableau provides a wide range of out of box visualization options. Bar chart and line chart are most normally used. Bar chart is good for comparing the data among different categories. Line chart is mostly used to see the trend overtime. We will deep dive into some advanced use cases of these two char types.

Now let's walk through an example of creating a stacked bar chart with lines that show percentage. This example is using the Superstore data source. The following steps need to be performed:

1. Create a view as shown in the following figure:

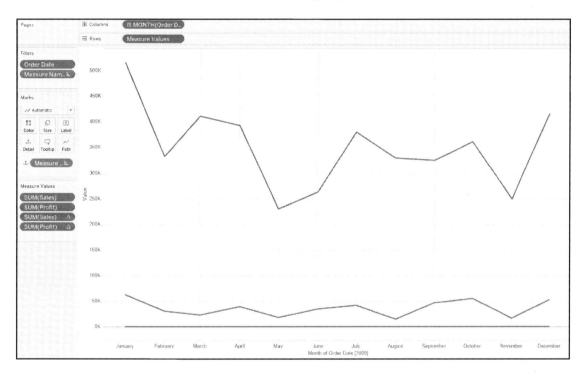

2. The measure values include **SUM (Sales)**, **SUM (Profit)**, and two table calculations as percentage of total for **SUM (Sales)** and **SUM (Profit)**. You can see that since the two table calculations are in percentage, they become very hard to see compared to that with **SUM (Sales)** and **SUM (Profit)**. To make the table calculations more visible, we can create a dual axis chart with **SUM (Sales)** and **SUM (Profit)** as bars and table calculations as lines.

3. Drag another **Measure Values** to **Rows**:

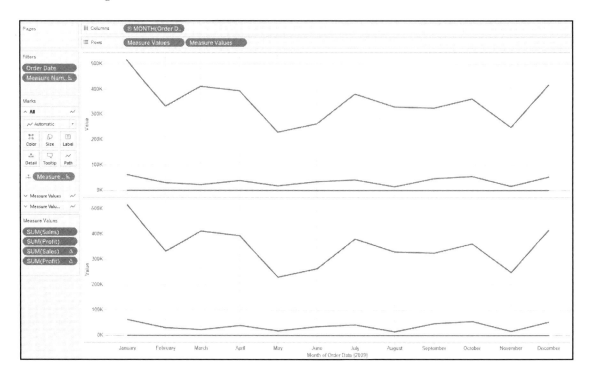

4. Add **Measure Names** to **Color**, change **top chart** to **bar chart**:

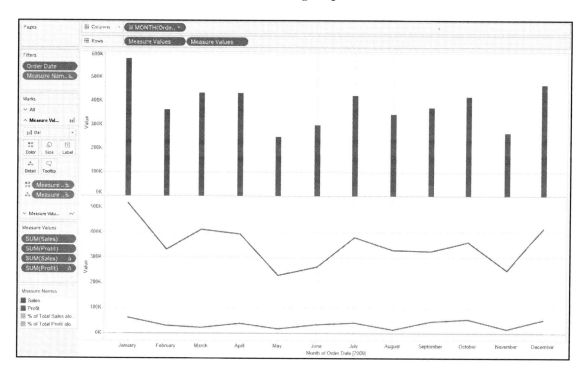

5. Select **Dual axis**:

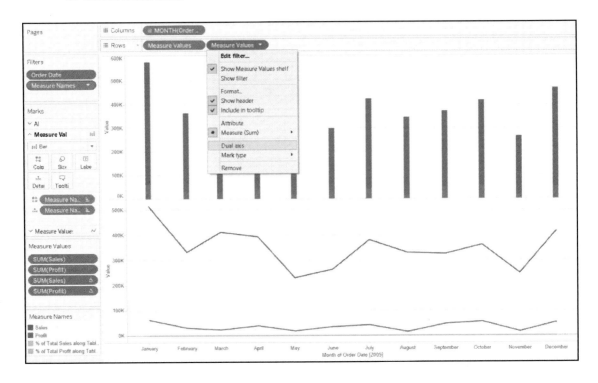

6. You will notice that the two table calculations of % of total are still hard to see. Take a look at the following figure:

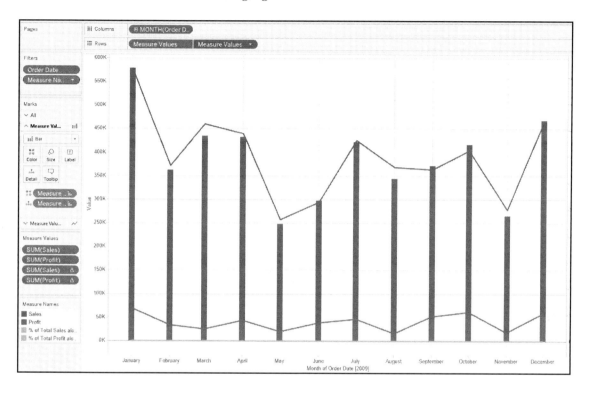

7. Now let's do the magic trick. Choose **Edit Axis** on the right and set it from 0 to 1:

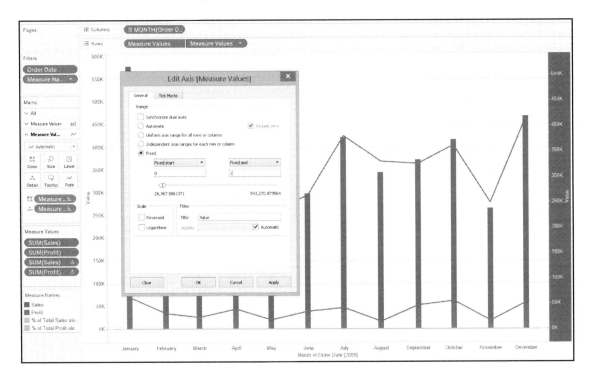

8. Now you will see the two table calculations of percentage of the total clearly in the view:

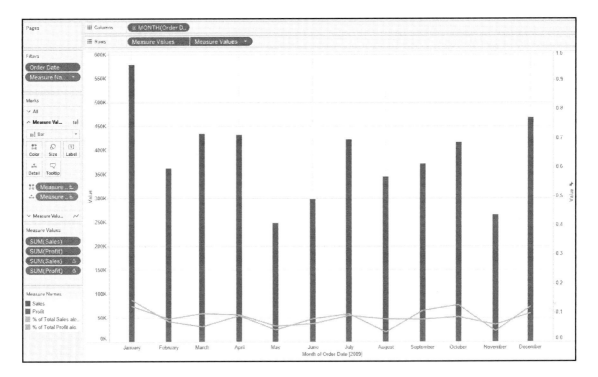

Treemap bar chart

Treemap is a very simple visualization but can give you a lot of insight. It is good to compare the measures among different categories.

Let's look at a cool example of adding treemap to a bar chart. I am using the Superstore data set. The following steps need to be performed:

1. Create a **Treemap** as shown in the following figure:

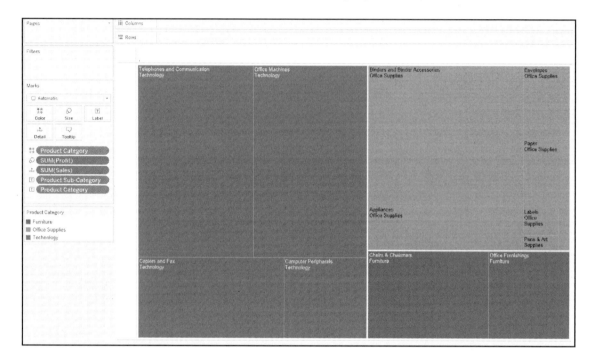

2. Press *Shift* and drag the **Product Sub-Category** to color; you will see that you have two dimensions in color:

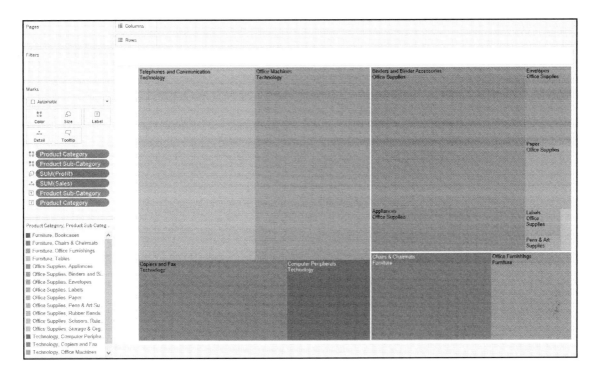

3. Drag **Product Category** to **Rows**. Now you will see that each bar of the bar chart is a **Treemap**, as shown next:

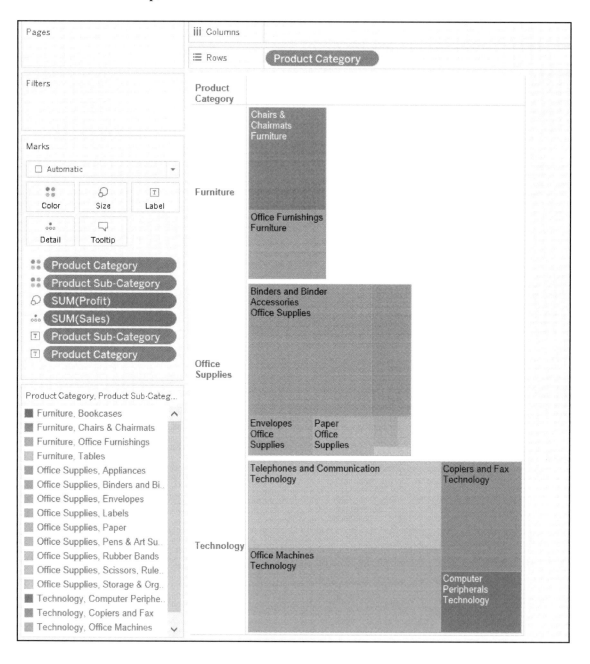

Stacked bar chart issue and workaround

Stacked bard chart can be used to divided data into certain bucket and do the analysis. But sometimes you may run into certain issues when using it. Now let's deep dive into what the issue is and the workaround to solve this issue.

You may already be familiar with using stacked bar charts and reference lines to show the total of measures while keeping the lower level of details in the view.

For example, using the Superstore data set, we can look at the number of customers broken into buckets based on their sales of the last order. The view is as follows:

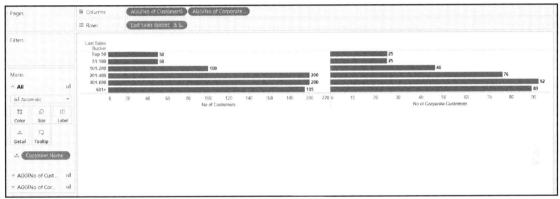

In this view, I have used the stacked bar to show the total number of customers in each last sales bucket while still keeping the customer name in the view. However, if I want to show the ratio of the number of corporate customers to the number of customers, I will have an issue, as shown in the following figure:

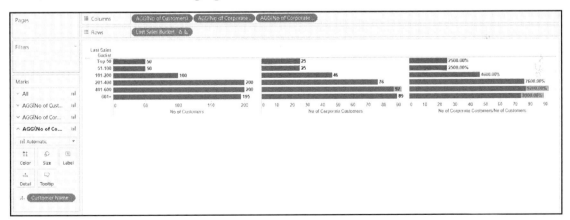

Since the customer name is in the view, the ratio is calculated for each customer. The workaround is to create a `Window_SUM` table calculation for the number of customers and the number of corporate customers and use the table calculation to calculate the ratio. Following are the steps to be performed to this end:

1. Create the following calculated fields:

2. This is the calculation for the number of customers:

```
!No of Customers                    Orders (Sample - Superstore Sales (Excel))

Results are computed along Table (Across).
CASE [Index]
WHEN 1 THEN WINDOW_SUM(IF [Last Sales Bucket] = "Top 50" THEN [No of Customers] END)
WHEN 2 THEN WINDOW_SUM(IF [Last Sales Bucket] = "51-100" THEN [No of Customers] END)
WHEN 3 THEN WINDOW_SUM(IF [Last Sales Bucket] = "101-200" THEN [No of Customers] END)
WHEN 4 THEN WINDOW_SUM(IF [Last Sales Bucket] = "201-400" THEN [No of Customers] END)
WHEN 5 THEN WINDOW_SUM(IF [Last Sales Bucket] = "401-600" THEN [No of Customers] END)
WHEN 6 THEN WINDOW_SUM(IF [Last Sales Bucket] = "601+" THEN [No of Customers] END)
END
```

3. This is the calculation for the number of corporate customers:

```
!No of Corporate Customers          Orders (Sample - Superstore Sales (Excel))

Results are computed along Table (Across).
CASE [Index]
WHEN 1 THEN WINDOW_SUM(IF [Last Sales Bucket] = "Top 50" THEN [No of Corporate Customers] END)
WHEN 2 THEN WINDOW_SUM(IF [Last Sales Bucket] = "51-100" THEN [No of Corporate Customers] END)
WHEN 3 THEN WINDOW_SUM(IF [Last Sales Bucket] = "101-200" THEN [No of Corporate Customers] END)
WHEN 4 THEN WINDOW_SUM(IF [Last Sales Bucket] = "201-400" THEN [No of Corporate Customers] END)
WHEN 5 THEN WINDOW_SUM(IF [Last Sales Bucket] = "401-600" THEN [No of Corporate Customers] END)
WHEN 6 THEN WINDOW_SUM(IF [Last Sales Bucket] = "601+" THEN [No of Corporate Customers] END)
END
```

4. This is the calculation of the ratio of the number of corporate customers to the number of customers:

5. This is the calculation to create the header for sales bucket:

```
!Last Sales Bucket Header        Orders (Sample - Superstore Sales (Excel))

CASE [Index]
WHEN 1 THEN "Top 50"
WHEN 2 THEN "51-100"
WHEN 3 THEN "101-200"
WHEN 4 THEN "201-400"
WHEN 5 THEN "401-600"
WHEN 6 THEN "601+"
END
```

6. Using the `Window_SUM` to calculate the ratio will resolve the issue. The final view is as follows:

Scatterplot

Most of you are familiar with the concept of scatterplot. It is used to show the relationships between different measures. But the traditional scatterplot may have some drawbacks in analyzing survey data. Now let me explain the drawbacks with an example.

For example, I have the following sample data from an HR survey, and I want to analyze the **EnvironmentSatisfaction** versus **JobSatisfaction**. Each variable has a scale of 1 to 4.

Age	Attrition	BusinessTravel	DailyRate	Department	DistanceFromHome	Education	EducationField	EmployeeCount	EmployeeNumber	EnvironmentSatisfaction	JobSatisfaction	Gender	HourlyRate
41	Yes	Travel_Rarely	1102	Sales	1	2	Life Sciences	1	1	2	4	Female	94
49	No	Travel_Frequently	279	Research & Development	8	1	Life Sciences	1	2	3	2	Male	61
37	Yes	Travel_Rarely	1373	Research & Development	2	2	Other	1	4	4	3	Male	92
33	No	Travel_Frequently	1392	Research & Development	3	4	Life Sciences	1	5	4	3	Female	56
27	No	Travel_Rarely	591	Research & Development	2	1	Medical	1	7	1	2	Male	40
32	No	Travel_Frequently	1005	Research & Development	2	2	Life Sciences	1	8	4	4	Male	79
59	No	Travel_Rarely	1324	Research & Development	3	3	Medical	1	10	3	1	Female	81
30	No	Travel_Rarely	1358	Research & Development	24	1	Life Sciences	1	11	4	3	Male	67
38	No	Travel_Frequently	216	Research & Development	23	3	Life Sciences	1	12	4	3	Male	44
36	No	Travel_Rarely	1299	Research & Development	27	3	Medical	1	13	3	3	Male	94
35	No	Travel_Rarely	809	Research & Development	16	3	Medical	1	14	1	2	Male	84
29	No	Travel_Rarely	153	Research & Development	15	2	Life Sciences	1	15	4	3	Female	49
31	No	Travel_Rarely	670	Research & Development	26	1	Life Sciences	1	16	1	3	Male	31
34	No	Travel_Rarely	1346	Research & Development	19	2	Medical	1	18	2	4	Male	93
28	Yes	Travel_Rarely	103	Research & Development	24	3	Life Sciences	1	19	3	3	Male	50
29	No	Travel_Rarely	1389	Research & Development	21	4	Life Sciences	1	20	2	1	Female	51
32	No	Travel_Rarely	334	Research & Development	5	2	Life Sciences	1	21	1	2	Male	80
22	No	Non-Travel	1123	Research & Development	16	2	Medical	1	22	4	4	Male	96
53	No	Travel_Rarely	1219	Sales	2	4	Life Sciences	1	23	1	4	Female	78
38	No	Travel_Rarely	371	Research & Development	2	3	Life Sciences	1	24	4	4	Male	45
24	No	Non-Travel	673	Research & Development	11	2	Other	1	26	1	3	Female	96
36	Yes	Travel_Rarely	1218	Sales	9	4	Life Sciences	1	27	3	1	Male	82
34	No	Travel_Rarely	419	Research & Development	7	4	Life Sciences	1	28	1	2	Female	53
21	No	Travel_Rarely	391	Research & Development	15	2	Life Sciences	1	30	3	4	Male	96
34	Yes	Travel_Rarely	699	Research & Development	6	1	Medical	1	31	2	1	Male	83
53	No	Travel_Rarely	1282	Research & Development	5	3	Other	1	32	3	3	Female	58
32	No	Travel_Frequently	1125	Research & Development	16	1	Life Sciences	1	33	2	1	Female	72
42	No	Travel_Rarely	691	Sales	8	4	Marketing	1	35	3	2	Male	48
44	No	Travel_Rarely	477	Research & Development	7	4	Medical	1	36	1	4	Female	42

I can build a traditional scatterplot, as shown next:

Since there are four possible values for each measure, all the employees that have the same value to both measures are overlapping each other, so a total of 16 points are displayed in the view. Our goal is to drill down the results into certain groups, such as department.

Now let's add **Department** to the view, add **CNTD (Employee Number)** to size, change **Environment Satisfaction** and **Job Satisfaction** to **discrete**. We now see that the measure values are broken into one point for each employee and color coded by department, as shown next:

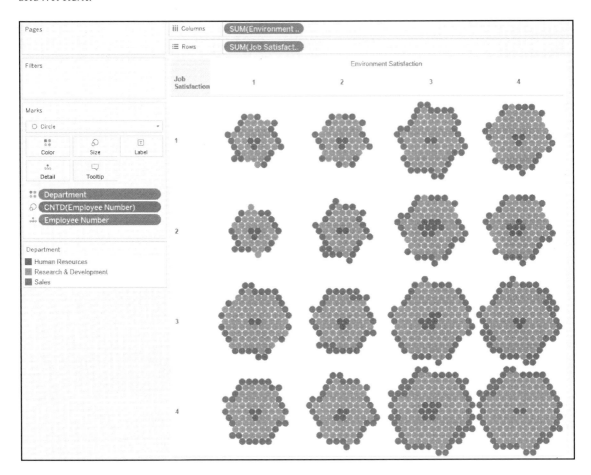

What if I want to add a trend line to the view? It is not possible in the preceding view since we are using discrete measures. The trick is to add a random number to the existing discrete measure and make them continuous.

1. Create the following two calculated fields:

```
Ajusted ES                    WA_Fn-UseC_-HR-Employee-Attriti (HR Survey)

Results are computed along Table (Across).
sum([Environment Satisfaction])
+ ((INT(((PREVIOUS_VALUE(MIN(DATEPART('second', NOW())))
* DATEPART('minute', NOW()) * DATEPART('hour', NOW()) * DATEPART('day', NOW()))))
  * 1140671485 + 12820163) % (2^24)) / (2^24) * 19) + 1)-19/2)/50
```

2. Change the view as follows, set the two measures to compute using **Employee Number**. Now you can add a trend line to the view since both the measures are continuous. This is shown in the following figure:

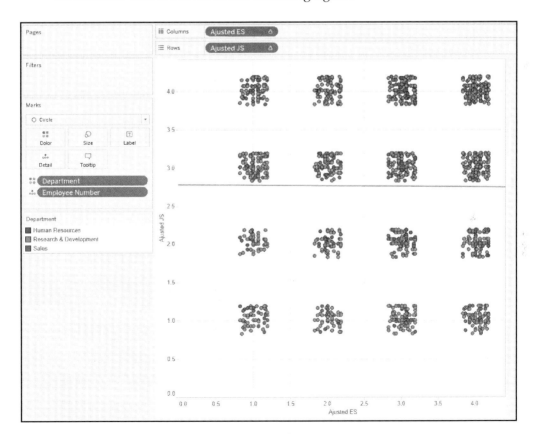

Waffle chart

Waffle chart is a chart in the shape of a square and with small squares inside the big square. It is used to show the percentage of certain category compared to all the categories. Now let's look at an example of creating a waffle chart to show percentage data.

To create a waffle chart, we need to create a data set for the waffle, which is a *10 x 10* grid.

The data to create the grid is as follows:

Column	Row
1.00	1.00
2.00	1.00
3.00	1.00
4.00	1.00
5.00	1.00
6.00	1.00
7.00	1.00
8.00	1.00
9.00	1.00
10.00	1.00
1.00	2.00
2.00	2.00
3.00	2.00
4.00	2.00
5.00	2.00
6.00	2.00
7.00	2.00
8.00	2.00
9.00	2.00
10.00	2.00
1.00	3.00
2.00	3.00
3.00	3.00
4.00	3.00
5.00	3.00
6.00	3.00
7.00	3.00
8.00	3.00
9.00	3.00
10.00	3.00
1.00	4.00
2.00	4.00
3.00	4.00
4.00	4.00
5.00	4.00
6.00	4.00
7.00	4.00
8.00	4.00
9.00	4.00
10.00	4.00

For each row (1-10), there are 10 columns (1-10). We will use these rows and columns to create the *10 x 10* grid.

1. Create a combined field to represent the cell in the grid:

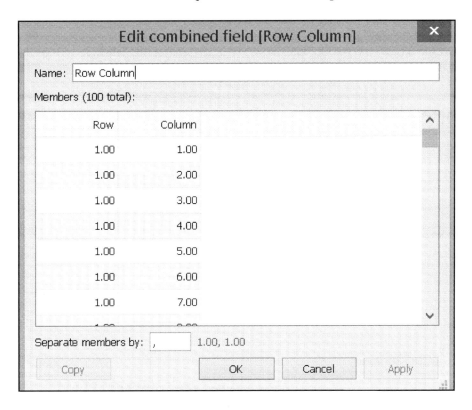

2. Create a profit ratio in the Superstore data set:

3. Create a calculated field in the **Waffle** data set to visualize the `Profit%` value in the 10 x 10 grid. We will create one calculation for each product category.

4. This is the calculation for `furniture` products:

5. This is the calculation for `technology` products:

6. This is the calculation for `office` products:

```
office                    Waffle
Results are computed along Table (Across).
if index()<=round(([Sample - Superstore Sales (Excel)].[Profit%],2)*100 then "color" else "no" end
```

7. Create a view for each **Product Category** as shown in the following figure, set **furniture** as **Compute using Row Column**, and use **Product Category** as a filter.

8. The view for **furniture** will be something as follows:

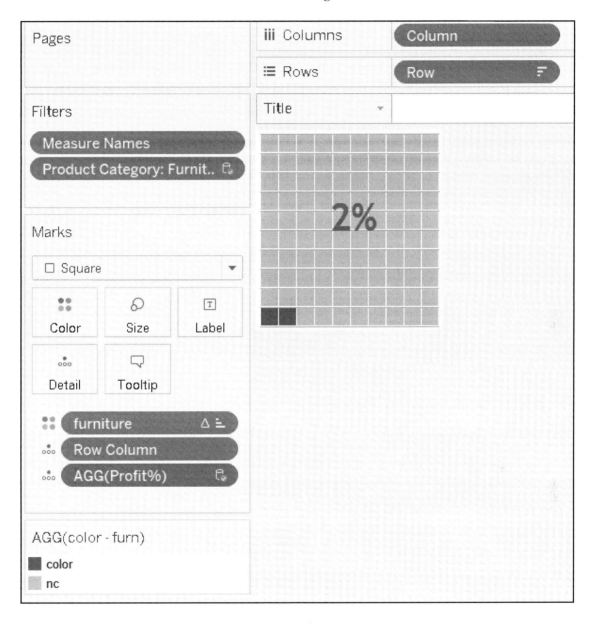

9. The view for **technology** will be something like this:

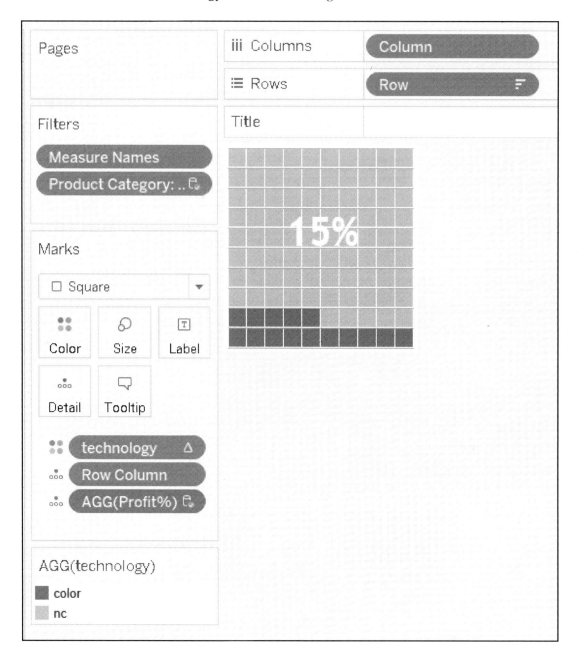

10. The view for **Office Supplies** will be something like this:

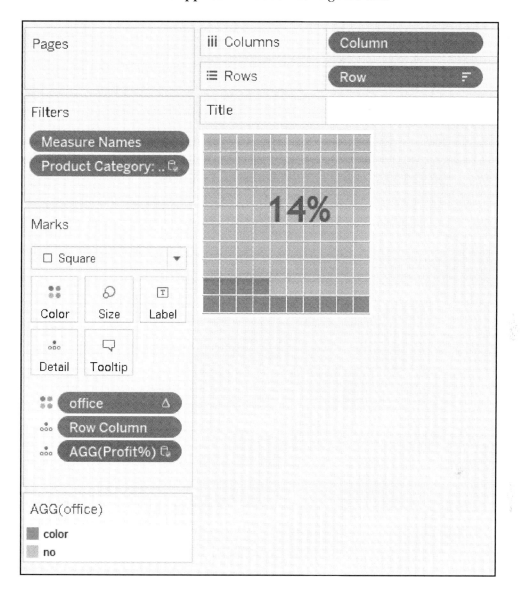

The final view is as follows:

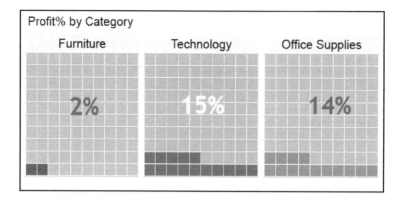

Jitter chart

Jittering is a very good technique used to separate data points that are overlapping each other in the view. Let's look at an example of creating a jitter chart. You have a data set of salaries from many people as shown next, and you want to let the user input their own salaries and compare with the salaries of others:

Gender	ID	Age	Salary
Female	1872	20	$23,000
Female	1467	20	$28,000
Female	1383	20	$31,000
Female	1977	20	$31,000
Female	679	20	$33,000
Female	1356	20	$34,000
Female	1229	20	$35,000
Female	2352	20	$35,000
Female	40	20	$37,000
Female	423	20	$37,000
Female	2175	20	$42,000
Female	2252	20	$44,000
Female	1466	20	$48,000
Female	221	20	$48,000
Female	366	20	$54,000
Female	470	21	$23,000

If we create a scatterplot as shown in the following figure, it is very hard to tell where you are since there are so many dots in one column:

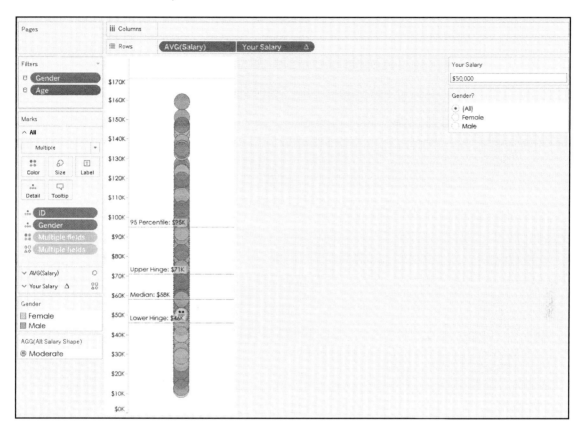

A solution is to jitter the dots and spread them in both directions, as follows:

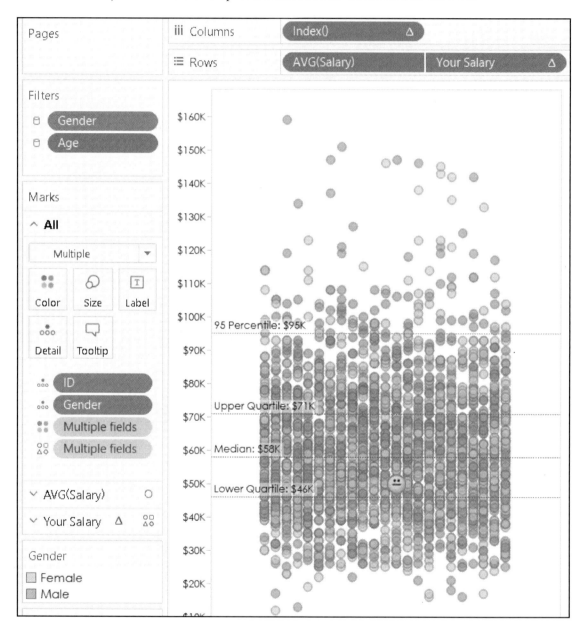

The way to spread the dots is to add an index value for each dot. So you are displaying the salary value on the *y* axis, and the *x* axis is showing the index value. We set the index to **compute using ID**. Since there is no relationship between ID and salary, the index is a random number.

Now that you understand why we want to jitter the Viz and how we do it, let's build the Viz:

1. Create a calculated field, as shown in the following figure, to be the index. Technically you can pick any prime number, but you can test out the number that is the best to display the data. This is shown next:

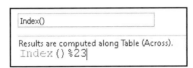

2. Create a view as follows. Set **Index** to **compute using ID**, and hide the header:

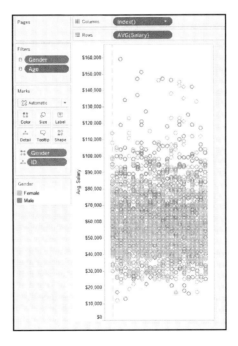

3. Create a parameter to let the user enter salary:

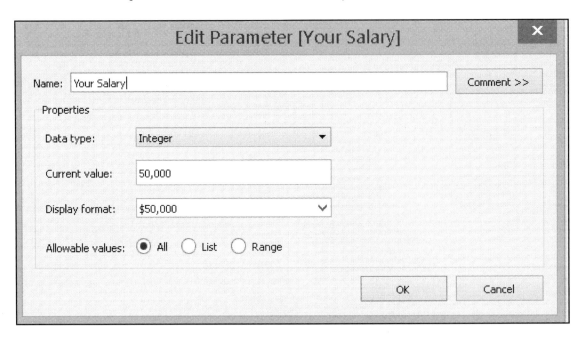

4. Create a calculated field to display the salary entered in the view. Since we use 23 to calculate the index number, we set the index for the salary entered as 12 so it can be displayed in the middle of the *x* axis. This is shown next:

Your Salary

Results are computed along Table (Across).
```
IF INDEX()==12 then
avg([Parameters].[Your Salary])
end
```

5. Create a calculated field to calculate the percentile of the entered salary among all the salaries in the data set:

```
Your Percentile

Results are computed along Table (Across).
1-
window_sum(sum(if ([Parameters].[Your Salary] )<([Salary]) then 1
else 0
end)/window_count(count([ID])))|
```

6. Create a calculated field to change the shape of the entered salary in the view:

```
Change Logo

If [Your Percentile]<=.25 then "Sad"
elseif [Your Percentile]<=.5 then "Moderate"
elseif [Your Percentile]<=.95 then "Pleased"
Else "Delighted"
end
```

7. Make sure you have the custom shape available in the My Tableau Repository
   | Shapes folder; name them accordingly:

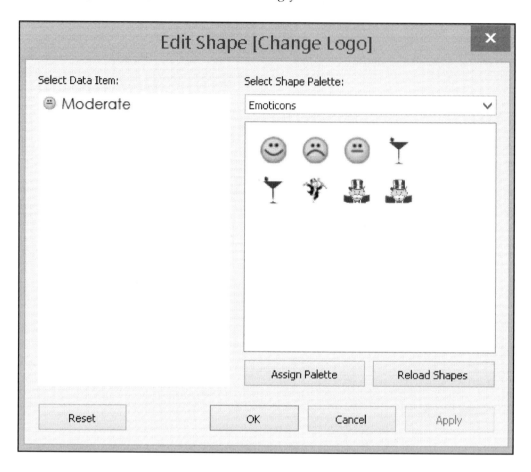

8. Add the **Your Salary** calculation to the view, choose **Dual axis**, then **synchronize axis**, and **hide the header**. Drag the **Change Log** calculation to the shape mark of **Your Salary**:

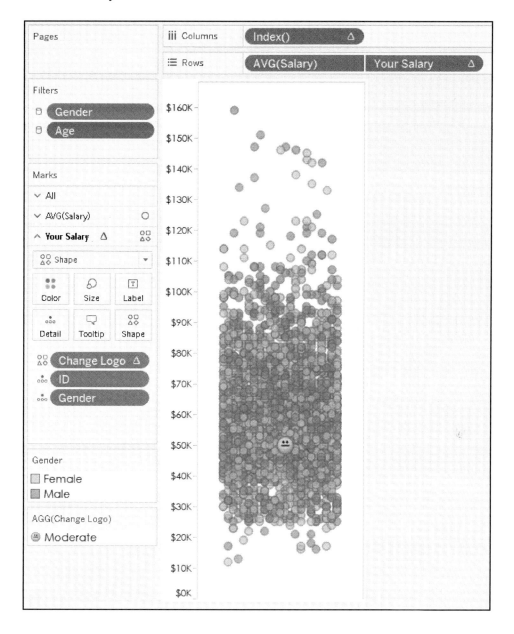

9. Lastly, add reference lines to show quartile and 95 percentile. The final view is as follows:

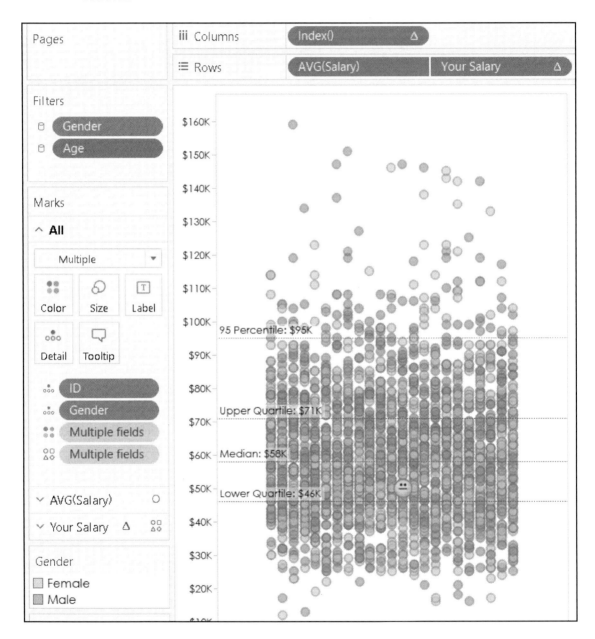

Circle chart

All of the dashboards we have seen are vertical and horizontal. Have you ever wanted to build a chart that is circular?

The following Viz in Tableau public is displaying countries in a circle:

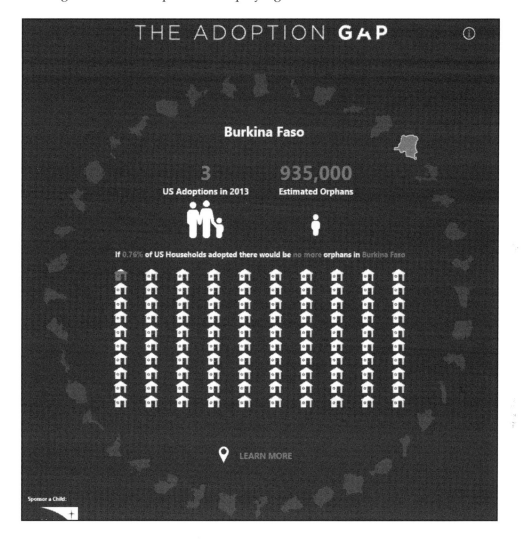

We can create a similar chart using the Superstore data set. For example, I want to look at the top *N* customers by sales in a circle. The following steps are to be performed:

1. Create a parameter to get the value for `Top N`:

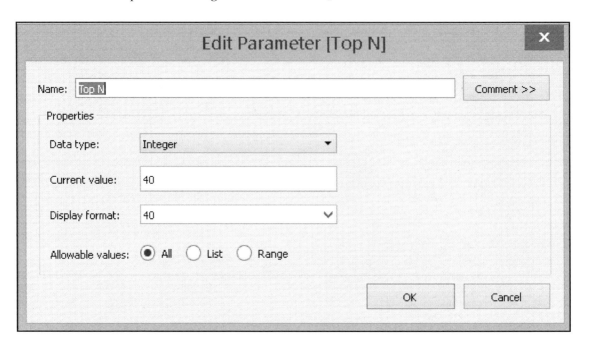

2. Create a calculated field to rank the sales:

3. Now we need to figure out the position of the top *N* customers. The center of the circle is (0, 0). We need to know what the (*x*, *y*) of the customer in the circle is, which means that we need to know the radians between each (*x*, *y*).

- You may not be familiar with what radian is. A circle is 360 degrees or 2 x PI radians. You can draw a circle by this formula, n x PI/(N/2). The *n* is the current point that you are drawing, such as point 1, point 2, ..., point *n*. In our case, it is the rank of sales. The *N* is the total number of points you are going to draw; in our case, it is the value of the parameter Top *N*.
- After we know the radians for each point, we know that the (x, y) for each point is calculated as: *x=sin (radians), y=cos (radians)*.
- Now you can create two calculated fields to get the (*x*, *y*) position of the customer:

- Create a **calculated field** to adjust the size of the shape based on the Top *N* number entered:

- Create the view as shown in the following figure, set the table calculation to **Compute using Customer Name**, use customer name as filter to get the Top *N* customers by **SUM (Sales)**:

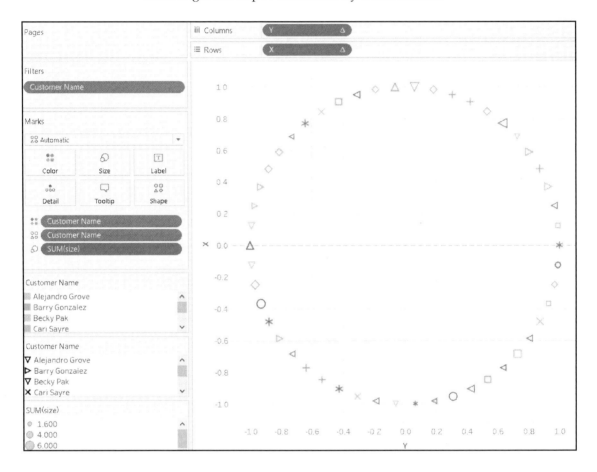

Network graph

Network graph is used to visualize the relationship between different points in the networks, such as social network. To create a network graph, you need to have a sample data set, as shown in the following figure.

These are the first seven columns of the data set:

Circle Y	Customer Type	Direction	ID	In Degree
9000	Corporate	In Degree	5	1
700	Corporate	In Degree	3	1
9000	Corporate	Out Degree	2	1
4000	Corporate	Out Degree	1	0
700	Corporate	Out Degree	7	1
5000	Personal	In Degree	9	3
5000	Personal	In Degree	2	3
5000	Personal	In Degree	6	3
8000	Personal	In Degree	4	1
3500	Personal	In Degree	1	2
3500	Personal	In Degree	7	2
4500	Personal	In Degree	8	1
7500	Personal	Out Degree	4	0

These are the next five columns of the data set:

Initiating Persion	Line X	Line Y	Node Name	Relationship
Wayne	3500	9000	Mary	Wayne-->Mary
Wayne	5500	700	Marjory	Wayne-->Marjory
Mary	3500	9000	Mary	Mary-->Jane
Ken	9500	4000	Ken	Ken --> Bill
Marjory	5500	700	Marjory	Marjory-->Bill
Bill	5000	5000	Jane	Bill-->Jane
Mary	5000	5000	Jane	Mary-->Jane
Sally	5000	5000	Jane	Sally-->Jane
Roger	7000	8000	Sally	Roger-->Sally
Ken	8000	3500	Bill	Ken --> Bill
Marjory	8000	3500	Bill	Marjory-->Bill
Jane	1200	4500	Wayne	Jane-->Wayne

These are the last seven columns of the data set:

Residence	Sales	Sales For Display	Secondary Person	Total Sales
CA	0	9,000	Mary	13,000
FR	0	20,000	Marjory	7,500
CA	13,000	*null*	Jane	13,000
DE	10,000	*null*	Bill	10,000
FR	7,500	*null*	Bill	7,500
DE	0	14,000	Jane	8,000
DE	0	13,000	Jane	8,000
DE	0	3,000	Jane	8,000
FR	0	5,000	Sally	3,000
USA	0	10,000	Bill	14,000
USA	0	7,500	Bill	14,000
USA	0	8,000	Wayne	29,000

1. Create a view as shown in the following figure by dragging **Line X** to **Rows** and **Line Y** to **Columns**, and then change **Mark Type** to **Circles**:

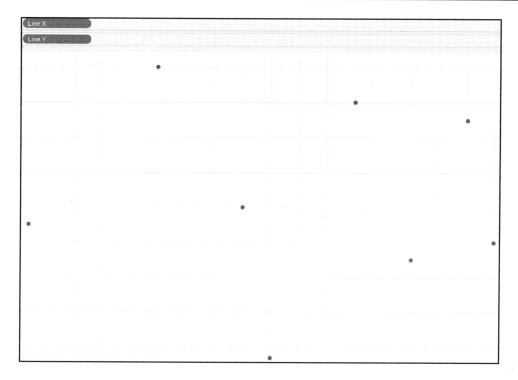

2. Add **Circle Y** to **Columns**, choose **Dual axis** and **Synchronize axis**:

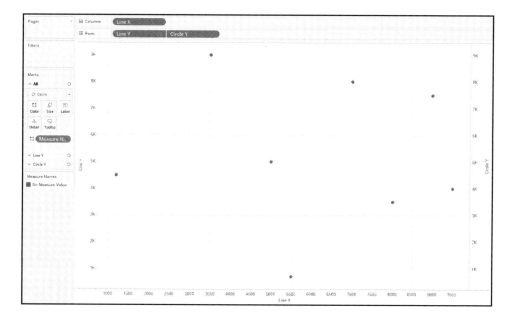

3. Set the **Circle Y** mark as **Pie**, color by **ID**, drag **Node Name** to **Label**, **ID** to **Level of Detail**, and make the **Pie** mark larger:

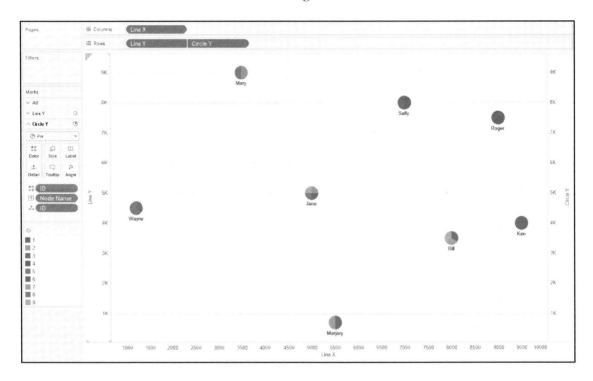

4. Edit the **Line Y** mark, drag **ID** and **Relationship** fields to **Level of Detail**, change **Mark Type** to **Line**, and make lines between nodes thinner:

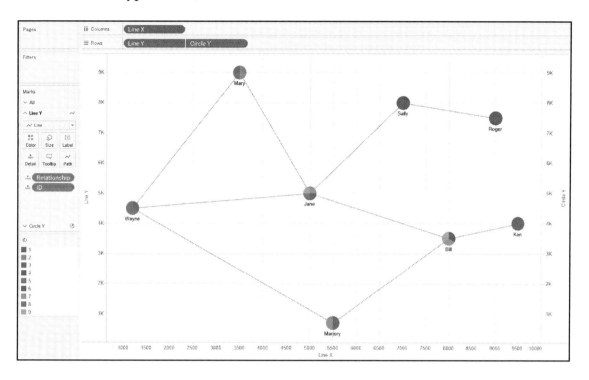

5. Uncheck **Show Header** in the **Line X**, **Line Y**, and **Circle Y** fields:

Calendar heat map

Heat map is a chart type that is used to compare different categories using different colors.

Now let's look at an example of how to create a heat map for the number of quarters it takes for customers to make another purchase after making the first purchase. I will use the Superstore data set for this example:

1. Create a calculated field as shown next to get the first purchase date for each customer:

```
1st Purchase Date                    [icon] Orders (Sample - Superstore Sales (Excel))

{FIXED [Customer Name]: MIN([Order Date])}
```

2. Create a calculated field to get the purchase dates other than the first one:

3. Create a calculated field to get the second purchase date for each customer:

4. Create a calculated field to get the quarter between the first purchase date and the second purchase date for each customer:

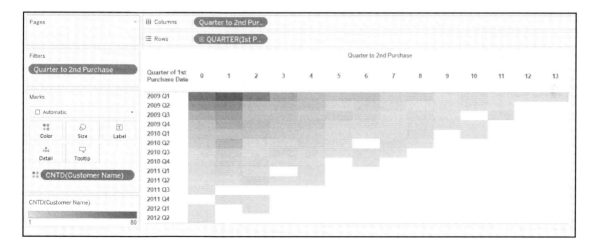

5. Build the heat map view as shown in the following figure, use a filter to exclude the **Quarter to 2nd Purchase** as **null**:

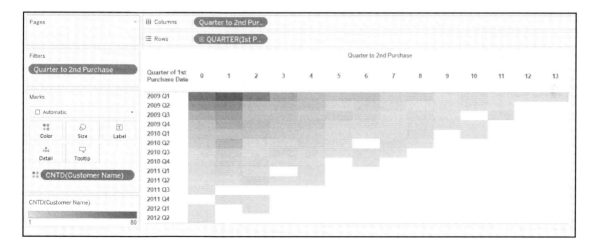

Multiple small maps

Sometimes you may need to show multiple maps in one visualization. There are two ways to create multiple small maps in Tableau. One is to create multiple individual maps as sheets and add them to a single dashboard. The other is to create a single sheet with multiple small maps. I will walk through the second way.

I will use the Coffee Chain data set for this example. We want to build a map of sales for each product type here:

1. Create the following calculated fields to get the row and column numbers for the small maps. Since there are four product types, we can create a 2×2 grid.

2. Create the following calculated fields to get the column and row numbers for each of the four maps. This is shown next:

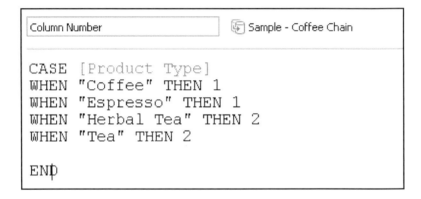

3. Add the **Column Number** and **Row Number** to the view, and change them to **dimension** and **discrete**, hide the header of column number and row number:

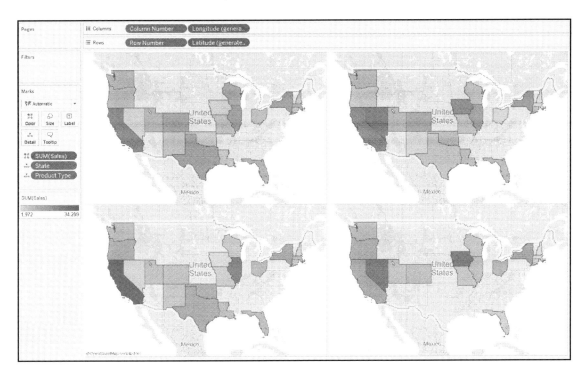

Now you have four small maps in one sheet, and each map is for one product type.

Cohort analysis

Before LOD calculation, doing cohort analysis was a pain since you needed to use custom SQL or other ways to create the customer start date if you did not have that date in the underlying data set, such as the Superstore data set. But with LOD calculation, we can easily create a calculation for the customer start date, and then do the cohort analysis.

I will walk you through two examples:

Example 1: How much revenue is generated by each cohort customer group?

1. First, create a calculated field as follows for `Customer Start Date`:

2. Create a view as follows to get the revenue generated by each customer cohort based on the start date:

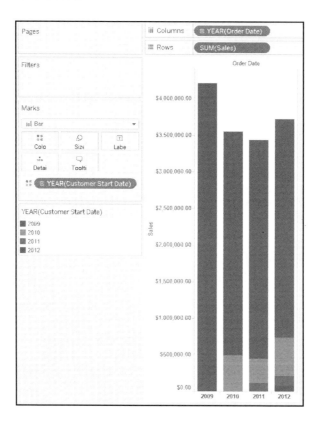

3. You can also change the **SUM (Sales)** to a table calculation of percentage of the total, **Compute using** and then select **Customer Start Date**:

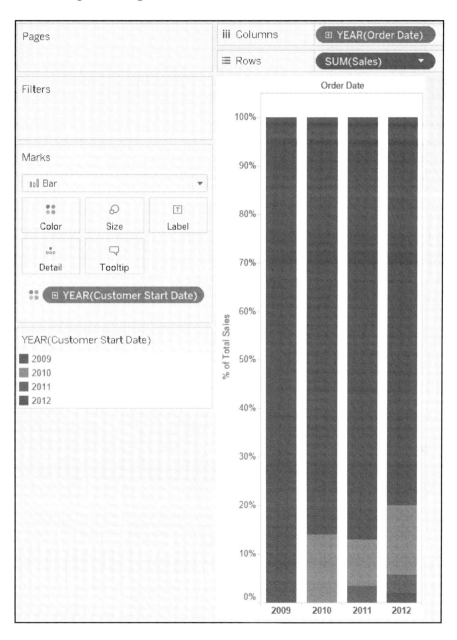

Example 2: What per cent of each customer cohort is purchasing at least *N* times?

1. Create a view as follows to get the number of customers in each cohort by **Customer Start Date**:

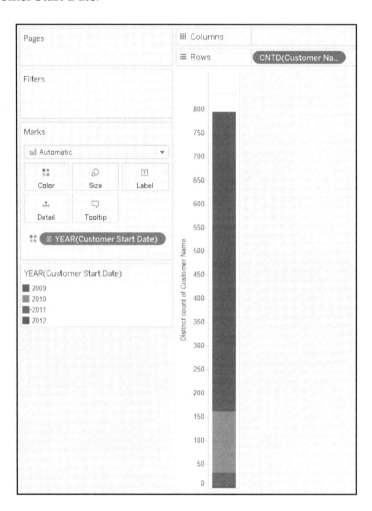

2. Create a calculation to get the number of orders per customer and change it to **discrete**:

```
{FIXED [Customer Name]: COUNTD([Order ID])}
```

3. Create a view as follows by adding `No of Orders Per Customer` to **Columns**:

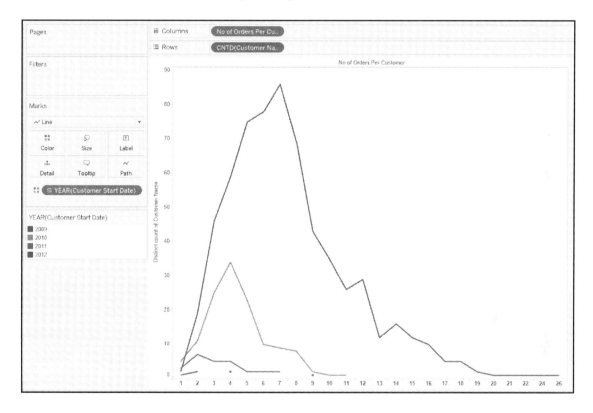

4. Change the **CNTD (Customer Name)** to the table calculation of running total:

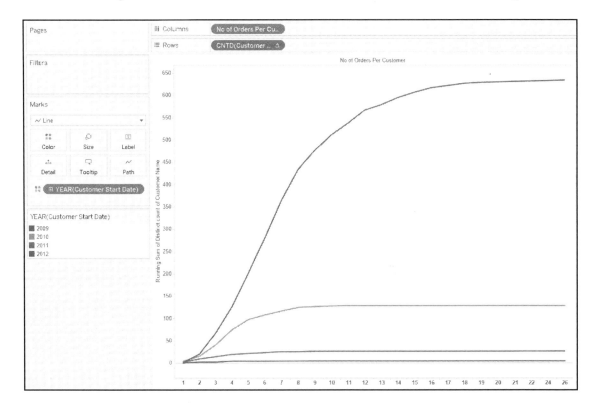

5. Add another table calculation to get the percentage of the total **Compute using No of Orders Per Customer**:

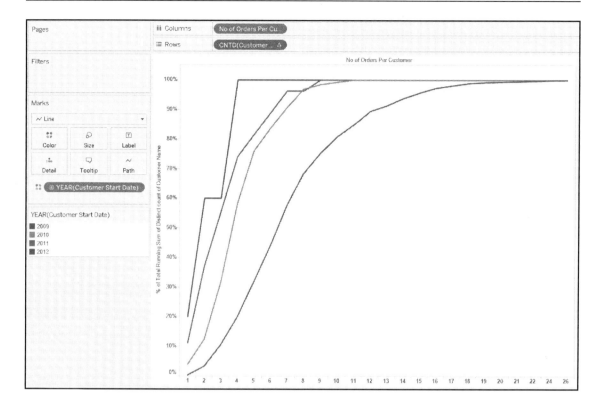

Visualize survey data

Now let discuss how to create visualization to analyze survey data.

Qualtrics web data connector

Qualtrics is a very popular survey tool. It has developed a web data connector to connect directly to Qualtrics survey data from Tableau.

Following are the steps to connect to Qualtrics data from Tableau:

1. Log into Qualtrics, and go to the survey you want to analyze.
2. Click on the **Responses** tab and select **Export Data**.
3. When the **Export Responses** box appears, click on **Tableau** and copy the URL.
4. Open **Tableau**, choose **New Data Source**, and select **Web Data Connector**.
5. When the **Web Data Connector** dialog box appears, paste the URL you just copied from Qualtrics.
6. Enter your Qualtrics username and password, and click on **log in**.
7. Qualtrics will ask you to select the fields you want to export/transpose; select the fields based on your needs.
8. When you are done selecting, click on **Import Survey Responses**.

Analyze different types of survey questions

This example is using the same HR survey data set used in the scatterplot example. Before analyzing the questions, let's look at the gender distribution to get a better understanding of the respondents:

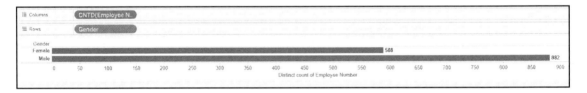

Now let's look at an example of a scale question.

Job Satisfaction has the 1-4 scale. We can look at the number of employees for each option:

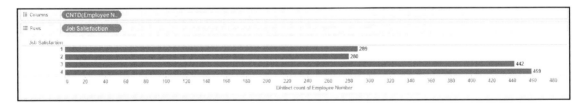

We can also look at the percentage of total responses for each option by adding a table calculation of percentage of the total:

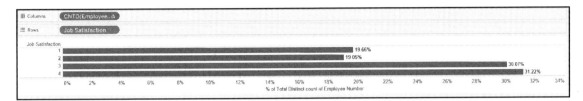

We can drill down the job satisfaction by gender:

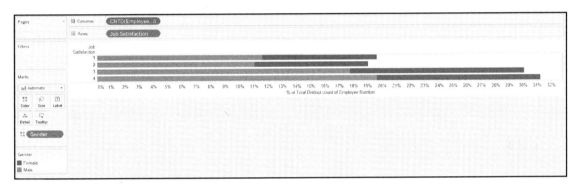

Now let's look by **Gender** and **Department** and what the distribution of job satisfaction looks like:

1. Set the **CNTD (Employee Name)** as **compute using Table (Across)**:

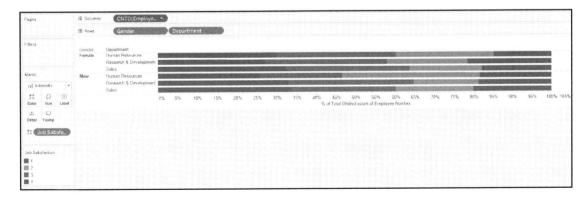

2. We can also add the average job satisfaction value to the view. Drag **Job Satisfaction** to the view and set as **average**. Change the mark type to **circle**:

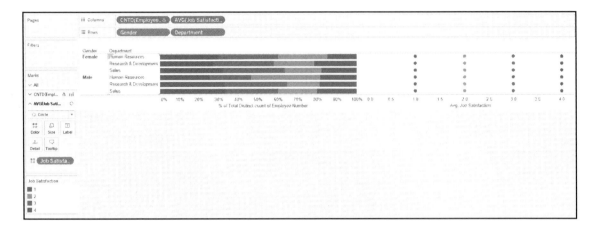

3. Remove the job satisfaction from the color of **Avg (Job Satisfaction)**:

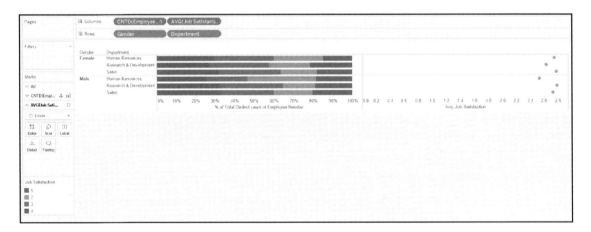

4. Choose **Dual Axis**, make the circle larger, and show mark label; change the axis range to allow the circle to be

5. closer to the middle, uncheck the **show header** option of both the measures:

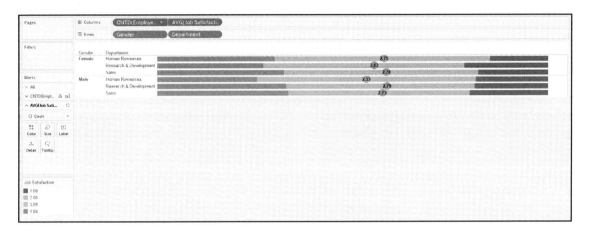

Summary

To summarize, you should keep in mind the following best practices for data blending: You should choose the best chart type to visualize your data based on your use case. You should try to be creative! There are so many ways to visualize data in Tableau. You should not forget to clean up your data, such as null value, before creating visualizations.

7
Dashboard

In the previous chapter, we talked about how to create different types of visualizations, such as bar charts, scatterplots, jitter charts, and so on. After building individual visualizations, we want to use them to create a dashboard that can tell stories and help get insights quickly. In this chapter, we will talk about tips, tricks, and the best practices for creating dashboards.

In this chapter, we will cover the following:

- The zen of dashboard design
- The five-second test of a dashboard
- Reviewing a dashboard
- Dashboard navigation
- Embedding YouTube videos
- Hiding things on Tableau dashboard

The zen of dashboard design

Here are some general guidelines on how to design a dashboard:

When designing a dashboard, you must keep in mind the importance of the following things, in that order: position is more important than color. Color is more important than size. Size is more important than shape.

What type of visualization do we use?

- If you have a dimension of time, use it on the x-axis
- If you have a dimension of location, use it on a map

- If you are trying to compare values, use a bar chart
- If you are trying to explore relationships between two dimensions, use a scatterplot
- If you are trying to find relative proportions of different groups, use a treemap

How do we create a great view?

- Emphasize the most important data-use position/color/size/shape
- Choose the right orientation
- Do not overload your view with too much information
- Organize your view in an intuitive way, normally following the logic of how you reach the conclusion of your analysis
- Limit the number of colors and shapes, normally no more than five different colors or shapes

How do we design the layout of the overall dashboard?

- Put the most important view at the top, normally the most important findings from your analysis
- Structure the interactivity from top to bottom or from left to right
- Limit the number of views on one dashboard to three or four, if possible
- Try not to use multiple color themes
- Try to put filters together
- If you have one legend for multiple views, put it close to those views
- Make sure the size for your view is right

How do we design interactivity?

Use color legend for highlighting. The best practices for filter are as follows:

- Think about what filters you want to show
- Pick the right filter type – quick filter/view as filter/filter action/parameter as a filter
- Try to use filters for all the views in the dashboard
- If your filters have a cascading effect, make sure to turn on the **Show Less Value button**
- Make sure the values in your quick filter are sorted in a reasonable way. For example, if your view shows products and their sales, instead of sorting the product alphabetically, sorting them by sales makes more sense.
- Remember that you do not need to have the filter field in the view

- Do not show the filter to users if you do not want them to change it
- A Slider filter is good for dates and numbers, list filter is good for categorical data
- Test your filters before publishing
- Check the default views before publishing

What are the final checks for the dashboard?

- Color
    - Try not to use more than two color palettes
    - Make sure there is no overlapping of colors
    - Use a light color for background
    - Think about how users will interpret your color
    - If the meaning of the color is hard to interpret, use a legend
    - Try not to use color coding for more than 12 distinct values

- Font
    - Use the following recommended fonts:
        - Verdana
        - Arial
        - Georgia
        - Tahoma
        - Time New Roman
        - Lucida sans
    - Calibri and Cambria are good for tooltips
    - Keep the following points in mind regarding the color of the font:
        - Axis and labels should be dark gray
        - Limit two-three font colors in the dashboard
    - Keep the font formatting consistent
    - Never change more than one attribute of a font (size, boldness, color, serif quality) for adjacent text

- Tooltips
    - Use the Calibri, Cambria, or Arial fonts
    - Use the most important part of the tooltip as the title
    - Make sure the measure names make sense
    - Make sure units are included in the tooltip

- Axis
    - Change your axis to be fixed if necessary

- Include gridline and reference line, if needed
- Make sure labels are appropriate and include units
- Make sure the label on tick marks are formatted appropriately
- Check mark labels

The five-second test of a dashboard

Here is a checklist of how to do a five-second test of your dashboard:

- The most important view goes at the top or the top-left
- Legends are close to their views
- Try not to use multiple color schemes on a single dashboard
- Provide interactivity
- Provide a title
- There should be an axis
- Provide key facts and figures
- Units have to be present
- Remove extra digits in numbers
- Provide great tooltips

Reviewing a dashboard

A great way to perfect your dashboard is to review it with your audience and get feedback from them. Here is a good way to conduct a dashboard review session:

- Have at least three reviewers
- Limit the meeting to 30 mins
- Send your dashboard to the reviewers before the meeting
- Test recommendations from reviewers during the meeting
- Ask the following questions:
    - What question does this dashboard answer?
    - Is this the best way to answer the question?
    - Does everything on the dashboard add value?
    - Does this dashboard apply visual best practice?
    - Is this dashboard right for its audience?

- Is there functional interactivity?
- Are labels, titles, and legends effective?

Dashboard navigation

Tableau provides very good navigation of switching dashboards using tabs. But sometimes the tabs are not easy enough to navigate when the users want to see a list of all the dashboards and go from dashboard to dashboard. We can solve this by adding a navigation dashboard.

I have a dataset, as shown next, which has the date and a link to my blog post of each day.

Date	Level	Link	Name
5/1/2016	Advanced	http://jennyxiaozhang.com/10-machine-learning-terms-in-simple-english/	10 Machine Learning Terms in Simple English
5/2/2016	Easy	http://jennyxiaozhang.com/performance-tableau-tipstricksbest-practices/	Performance – Tableau Tips, Tricks, Best Practices
5/3/2016	Advanced	http://jennyxiaozhang.com/6-things-you-need-to-know-about-spark/	6 Things You Need To Know About Spark
5/4/2016	Medium	http://jennyxiaozhang.com/visualization-tableau-tipstricksbest-practices/	Visualization – Tableau Tips, Tricks, Best Practices
5/5/2016	Advanced	http://jennyxiaozhang.com/4-things-you-need-to-know-about-yarn/	4 Things You Need To Know About YARN
5/6/2016	Medium	http://jennyxiaozhang.com/tableau-tipstricksbest-practices-formatting/	Tableau Tips, Tricks, Best Practices – Formatting
5/7/2016	Medium	http://jennyxiaozhang.com/tableau-tipstricksbest-practices-sortfilter/	Tableau Tips, Tricks, Best Practices – Sort/Filter
5/8/2016	Advanced	http://jennyxiaozhang.com/tableau-tipstricksbest-practices-calculation/	Tableau Tips, Tricks, Best Practices – Calculation
5/9/2016	Advanced	http://jennyxiaozhang.com/tableau-tipstricksbest-practices-data-blending/	Tableau Tips, Tricks, Best Practices – Data Blending
5/10/2016	Medium	http://jennyxiaozhang.com/tableau-tipstricksbest-practices-data-extract/	Tableau Tips, Tricks, Best Practices – Data Extract
5/11/2016	Easy	http://jennyxiaozhang.com/tableau-tipstricksbest-practices-basic-concepts/	Tableau Tips, Tricks, Best Practices – Basic Concepts
5/12/2016	Advanced	http://jennyxiaozhang.com/nosql-hbase-vs-cassandra-vs-mongodb/	NoSQL – HBase vs Cassandra vs MongoDB
5/13/2016	Medium	http://jennyxiaozhang.com/64-useful-excel-tricks-and-shortcuts/	64 Useful Excel Tricks and Shortcuts
5/14/2016	Advanced	http://jennyxiaozhang.com/6-things-you-need-to-know-about-hadoop/	6 Things You Need To Know About Hadoop
5/15/2016	Null	http://jennyxiaozhang.com/mobile-video-ads-is-the-real-future/	Mobile + Video = Winning Digital Marketing
5/16/2016	Null	http://jennyxiaozhang.com/digital-marketing-quick-and-easy-recipes/	Digital Marketing Quick and Easy Recipes
5/17/2016	Null	http://jennyxiaozhang.com/videos-must-watch-for-tech-lovers-forever/	Videos Must watch for Tech lovers
5/18/2016	Easy	http://jennyxiaozhang.com/tableau-google-analytics-dashboards/	Tableau Google Analytics Dashboards
5/19/2016	Easy	http://jennyxiaozhang.com/tableau-dashboards-and-storypoints-try-it/	Tableau Dashboards and Storypoints
5/20/2016	Easy	http://jennyxiaozhang.com/the-state-of-big-data-2014/	The State of Big Data 2014
5/21/2016	Easy	http://jennyxiaozhang.com/big-data-big-messy-data/	Big Data – Big Messy Data
5/22/2016	Null	http://jennyxiaozhang.com/success-what-is-your-definition/	Success – What is your definition?
5/23/2016	Null	http://jennyxiaozhang.com/why-all-leaders-should-post-on-linkedin/	Why All Leaders should post on LinkedIn
5/24/2016	Null	http://jennyxiaozhang.com/	About Me
5/25/2016	Null	http://jennyxiaozhang.com/impossible-list/	My Impossible List
5/26/2016	Null	http://jennyxiaozhang.com/infographic-resume/	Infographic Resume
5/27/2016	Null	http://jennyxiaozhang.com/places-ive-been/	Places I've Been
5/28/2016	Null	http://jennyxiaozhang.com/contact/	Contact Me
5/29/2016	Null	http://jennyxiaozhang.com/resume/	Resume
5/30/2016	Null	http://jennyxiaozhang.com/blog/	Blog
5/31/2016	Null	http://jennyxiaozhang.com/shuffle-the-ads-the-perfect-mix-makes-you-enjoy-more-relevant-ads/	Shuffle the Ads

The goal is to build a calendar format navigation dashboard. For each date, there is a button that users can click on and go to a blog post.

First, let's build the button using the following steps:

1. Create a calculated field as the **Header** for the button:

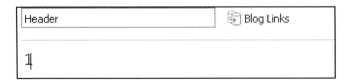

2. Drag the **Header** calculated field to **Columns**, change to **dimension**. Change the mark type to **shape**, and pick the arrow shape. Adjust the shape size:

3. Edit the axis to a fixed 0 to 5:

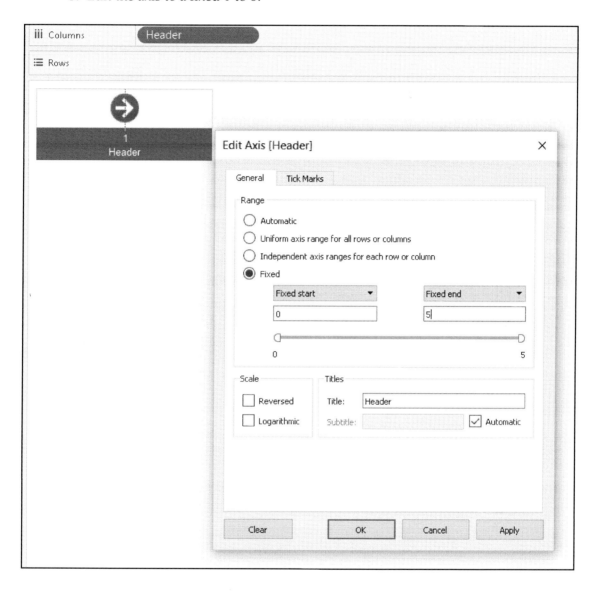

4. Uncheck **Show header**.
5. Create a view as shown in the following screenshot. Click on the last **Header** on **Rows** and choose **Dual axis**. Uncheck **Show header** for all dimensions/measures except **MONTH (Date)**, and **WEEKDAY (Date)**. Configure the marks as shown next. Change the shape to arrow.
6. Configure the first Header as shown in the following screenshot:

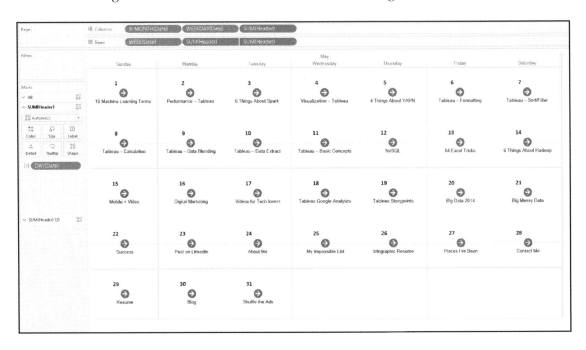

7. Configure the second Header, as follows:

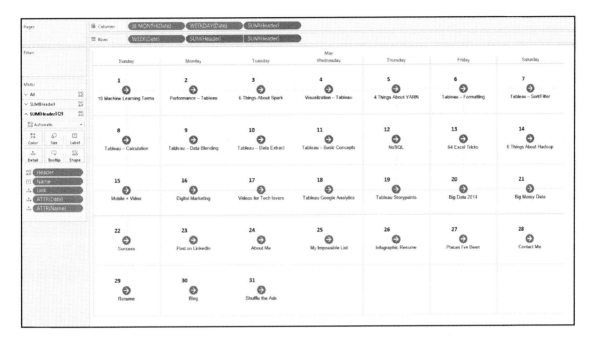

8. Add a sheet to a dashboard. Create a URL dashboard action, as follows:

Embedding YouTube videos

It is very simple to add YouTube videos to your Tableau dashboard; perform the following steps:

1. Go to the YouTube video that you want to share, and click on **Share-Embed**. Copy the URL of the video:

2. Create an Excel sheet with the information for each video. The URL is required:

Name	URL
Tips and Tricks from a Tableau Jedi	https://www.youtube.com/embed/IDyMMPiNVGw?list=PL-BWnq0WZ3JA6IxEzYfe5p3Sii1zv4yio
How to "Excel" with Tableau	https://www.youtube.com/embed/I0JRzPWjX9M?list=PL-BWnq0WZ3JA6IxEzYfe5p3Sii1zv4yio
Think Data Thursday: LoD of the Rings	https://www.youtube.com/embed/TWnC8sC8uOI?list=PL-BWnq0WZ3JA6IxEzYfe5p3Sii1zv4yio
Think Data Thursday: Tableau - How Did I Not Know That?	https://www.youtube.com/embed/KUpWAuTFCbQ?list=PL-BWnq0WZ3JA6IxEzYfe5p3Sii1zv4yio

3. Create a simple sheet with the Excel sheet. Make sure you have the URL in the view:

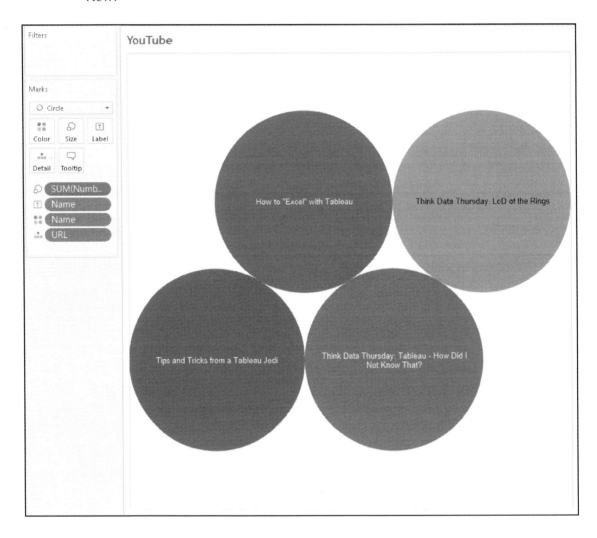

4. Add the sheet to a dashboard. Drag the web page to the dashboard, and leave the **Edit URL** box blank. Click on **OK**:

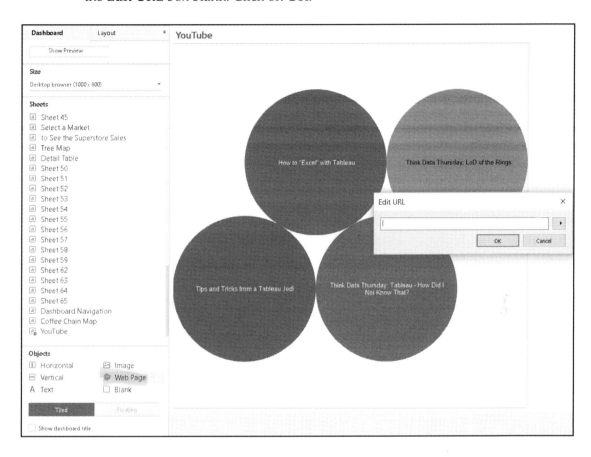

4. Add a dashboard URL action, as follows:

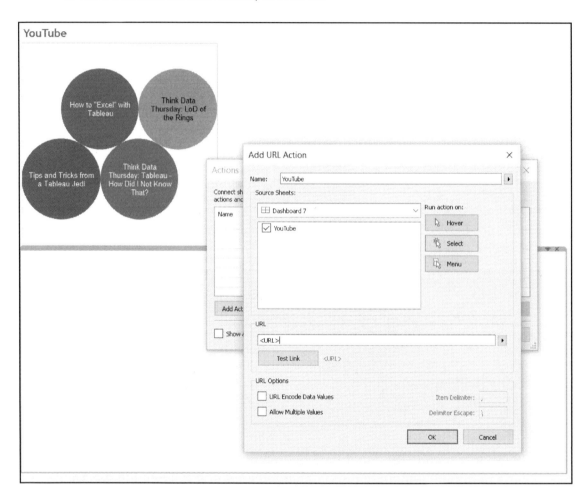

5. When you select a video on the top sheet, you will see the video loaded in the bottom web page box:

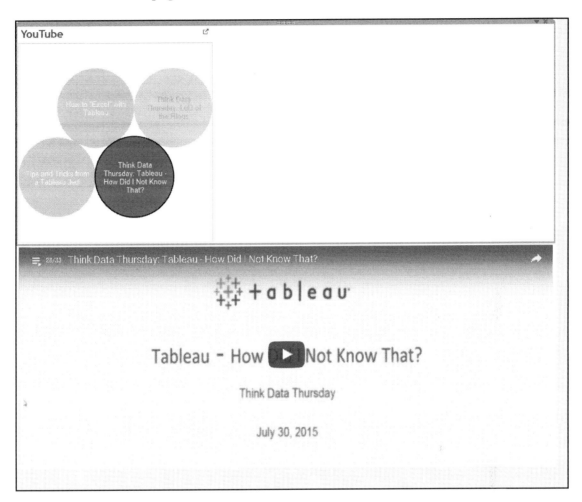

Hiding information on a Tableau dashboard

Sometimes you may want to add something to a Tableau dashboard that only can be seen by you, not the end users.

For example, you may want to add the five-second dashboard test checklist to your dashboard so you can remind yourself to go through the test before publishing it. Or you may want to add some instructions on how to set default filters and parameters.

Here is the trick on how to do it.

When you want to add the hidden item to your dashboard, add it as a floating item, and then use the position control in the bottom-left corner to change the position of the item on the dashboard:

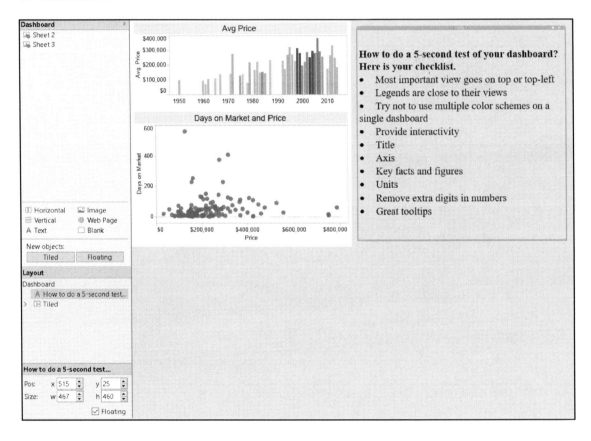

Once you publish the dashboard, you will not be able to see the hidden item:

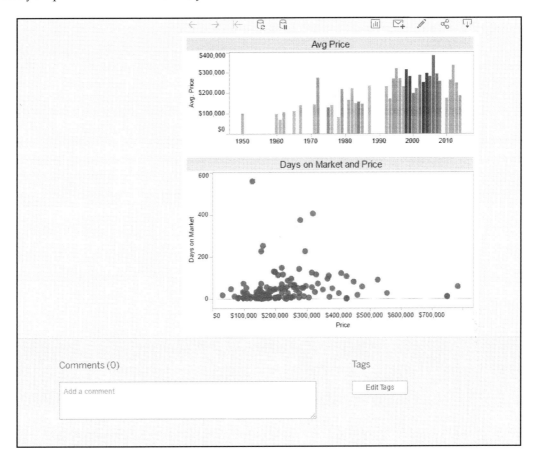

Summary

In summary, you should keep in mind the following best practices for data blending. You should understand and apply the Zen of dashboard design to your Tableau dashboards. You need to remember the sequence of importance for building dashboards: position is more important than color. Color is more important than size. Size is more important than shape. You should remember to conduct a five-second test of your dashboard. You should follow the dashboard review best practices to make your dashboard review sessions more productive. You need to be creative and integrate Tableau with other useful data sources.

8
Performance

In the previous chapter, we talked about how to create effective and impactful dashboards. In this chapter, we will talk about the tips and tricks you can use to improve the performance of your dashboards, such as reducing dashboard loading time.

In this chapter, we will cover the following:

- Auto update
- Filter
- Calculation
- Data extract
- Blending and Join
- Data source
- Dashboard

Auto update

If your Tableau reports are using very large data sets, and the performance does not meet your expectations, one trick is to try stopping Auto Update Worksheet. It is okay to keep the auto-update quick filter if the performance is not affected by it. Build your views by pausing auto-update, and start auto-update again once you finish building the view.

 If you stop the auto update on the dashboard, it will also stop the auto update worksheet for all the worksheets on the dashboard.

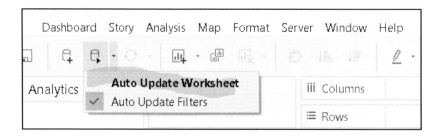

Filter

You can add filters first to limit the number of records shown in the visualization. After building the view, remove the filters to include all the data. This is very useful when trying to test out some calculated fields and table calculations.

Filters can help improve performance by reducing the data size, but complex filters can also use a lot of computation power and affect performance. So try to limit the number of filters used.

Keep only filters normally perform better than `Exclude` Filters. Exclude Filters need to load all the data from the dimension in order to exclude unwanted hits, so they need more time than keep only filters.

Context filters can help improve performance only when it can significantly reduce the amount of data to be used. The following are some general rules when using context filters to improve performance:

- If one context filter can significantly reduce the amount of data used, it is much better to use just one context filter than many. If a context filter does not reduce the size of the data set by 10% or more, it actually has a negative impact on the performance since the cost of computing the context filter is more than the data it reduces.
- Make all of your changes to the meta data before adding a context filter. Each time you change the metadata, such as converting dimensions to measures, Tableau will have to calculate the context filter again.
- Add the context filter before adding fields to other shelves. After adding the context filter, the queries that are run when you add fields to other shelves are much faster.
- If you want to add a date field as a context filter, you can use it as a continuous date. But context filters using date part such as YEAR (date) or on discrete dates are much more effective.
- If the dataset you are using has a lot of index, the context filter may have a negative impact on the performance.

Calculation

If the table calculations are of the DATE or DATETIME data type and are addressing along the dates, Tableau starts padding the domain. Tableau will generate a row for every combination of dimensions and all of the dates, not just the dates that go with the dimension. Domain padding on dates will have a significant negative impact on performance. A workaround for this is to create a string field for the date. Use the string instead of the date in the view, and set the compute using to the string.

Try to simplify your calculations. The sequence of performance is Boolean | Number | Date | String. For example, instead of using If SUM(Sales) >0 Then "True" Else "False" End, use SUM(Sales) >0.

Sometimes using `TOTAL()` can have a bad impact on performance. Try to use `WINDOW_SUM()` instead of `TOTAL()`.

Instead of using `WINDOW_SUM(SUM([Sales]))`, use `IF (FIRST()==0) THEN`

`WINDOW_SUM(SUM([Sales])) END`. You will get the same result, but Tableau will only calculate the table calculation once.

Data extract

When you are creating an extract, try to limit the size of the extract by applying filters to exclude data that you don't need, or aggregate data to certain level. You can also reduce the extract size by hiding unused fields. If you add calculations to the extract, optimizing the extract can improve performance.

The following optimizations can be done:

- Materialized calculated fields: Calculated fields will be calculated in advance and stored in the extract. When you are querying the extract, Tableau can look up the already calculated values rather than doing the calculation again.

    However, the following types of calculated fields are not materialized:

    - Calculations that use unstable functions, such as `NOW()` and `TODAY()`
    - Calculations that use external functions, such as `RAWSQL` and `R`
    - Table calculations

    If the calculation for a materialized calculation is changed or the calculation is deleted from the data source, the materialized calculation is removed from the extract until the extract is optimized again.

- **Acceleration views**: If a workbook has filters that are set to show only relevant values, calculating the values for that filter can cost a lot of computing resources. For this type of filters, Tableau has to evaluate the other filters in the workbook, and then calculate the filter values based on the values of other filters. To improve the performance for these filters, a view can be created that calculates the possible filter values and caches the values so Tableau can look up the view faster.

You can optimize the extract, as follows:

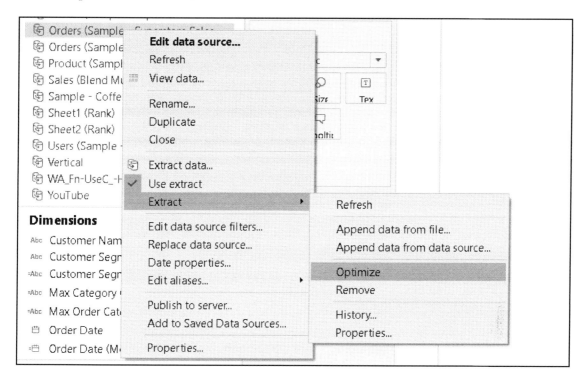

Blending and Join

Try to limit the number of joins. If you need many tables in a workbook, you may want to create separate data connections with joins, which are used to each worksheet in the workbook. Try not to perform data blending on dimensions that have many unique values because data blending is done in-memory. Try not to blend on strings since string queries and comparison cost a lot of computing resources.

Data source

A lot of the performance issue is caused by the underlying data source. So try to optimize your data source as much as possible.

If you connect to a data source with native database drivers, the performance is often better than the ODBC connector.

Try not to use custom SQL. Custom SQL is normally slower than queries created by Tableau because Tableau cannot optimize custom SQL queries. If custom SQL is definitely needed, use an extract so that the query only needs to run once. Also, limiting the parameters in custom SQL can improve performance.

If soft referential integrity is supported by your databases, using the Assume Referential Integrity option can improve the performance of inner joins.

Visualization

Try not to use a lot of marks. The more marks you have, the longer it takes to load the visualization. Limit the number of fields on the detailed text tables. Minimize the size of images or custom shapes. As a general rule of thumb, keep images of size under 50kb. If you are using custom shapes, transparent background PNGs perform better than JPGs.

Dashboard

Try to limit the number of worksheets on a dashboard. If you have more than four visualizations on a dashboard, the performance is likely to be worse. Automatic sizing is less efficient than fixed-size dashboard. So use a fixed size dashboard if possible.

Summary

In summary, you should keep in mind the following best practices for data blending. You should optimize underlying data sources before pulling them into Tableau. You should use data extracts instead of a live connection, when possible, and optimize it. You should limit your data size and only pull the minimum data needed for your analysis. You should simplify calculations, such as using Boolean calculation type instead of string, if possible. You should limit the number of filters and use context filter only if you can reduce 10% or more data. You should limit the number of joins and blending. You should limit marks and image size and use transparent background PNG images. You should limit the number of visualizations on a dashboard and use fixed-size.

9
Permission

In the previous chapter, we talked about how to improve the performance of your Tableau workbooks. In this chapter, we will talk about how to set permissions to make sure the users can see only the data that they are allowed to see.

In this chapter, we will cover the following:

- Permission hierarchy
- Inherit permissions in permission hierarchy
- Best practices

Permission hierarchy

There are six levels of permissions: site, project, group, user, workbook, and data source. This chart has the overview of the permission hierarchy:

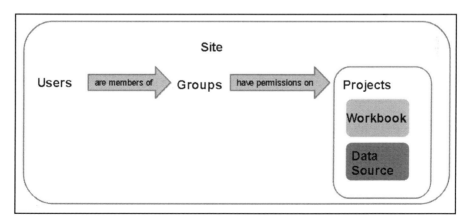

Now let's walk through each of them to understand how Tableau permissions work and interact with each other.

Sites

Each site is administered separately and has its own groups, users, projects, workbooks, and data sources. A user with permissions to some sites on a server will not have access to the other sites. They will not be able to log in or view any information on the sites they do not have permission to. That is why we have All Users and Site Users in the admin panel. If a user has permissions to multiple sites, they will be asked to choose which site they want to see when they log in to the server. After installation of Tableau, a site called Default will be created. You can rename it but cannot delete it since a server must always have at least one site.

Projects

Projects are also used to separate content in the server. However, as they share groups and users with the other projects on the same site, this is typically used as a way to separate the content into functional areas. For example, you may have Tableau users in finance, marketing, sales, and customer support and want to have different dashboards for each department. Projects are a great way of doing this. After installation of Tableau, a project will be created in the default site called "Default". You can rename it but cannot delete it since a site must always have a default project.

Access to a project is set by the permissions on it. A group or user can be assigned a set of permissions within the project to determine what they can or can't do with workbooks published to that project.

Groups

Groups are collections of users. Groups can be either manually created or synced from an Active Directory. Each site has at least one group called All Users, which comprises all the users on a site.

Users

Users are the individual users. Each user on Tableau Server must have a license type even if they are unlicensed. Each user can have two types of user rights: publish and administrator. When setting a user as administrator, you need to choose whether they are a system admin (can administer all sites and permissions) or site admin (can administer some sites and permissions).

Workbooks and data sources

Permissions set directly to workbooks or data sources are the most powerful ones. These permissions will overpower all other permissions within a site. When publishing, if the publisher sets permissions that users A-X have access to the workbook, even though the project says users A-X do not have access to the workbook, those permissions set by the publisher wins, so users A-X will have access to the workbook. However, if the publisher sets permissions that these users do not have access to the data source, the users will be able to see the workbook, but it will be blank because they don't have permission to see the data.

The permission hierarchy is like this:

Data source permissions > workbook permissions > group permissions > project permissions > site permissions.

For example, if the site permissions say that user X does not have access to any workbooks, any of the other permissions will overpower that site permission since it is at the lowest level.

Once you understand the permission hierarchy, here are some tips:

- Make sure the projects, users, and groups you set up can give everything the user needs without customizing each user's permission on the workbook level.
- Make sure Tableau Desktop users, who will be publishing dashboards and/or data sources, understand Tableau permissions and their responsibility in setting them.
- Limit the fields users can access in the underlying data source using views to prevent sensitive data from being accidentally published.
- If some data is very sensitive but needs to be visualized by certain people, create separate sites to limit who can see those visualizations.
- System and site administrators can see all data and visualizations within the server and site. So give these roles to only those people who are entitled to see all the data.

Inherit permissions in permission hierarchy

The "Inherit" option looks at the next level of permissions in the permission hierarchy and just takes those permissions. For example, if the workbook view permission is set as inherit, Tableau will look to the group permissions. If the group permissions are also set as inherit, Tableau will look at project permissions and all the way up to site permissions. If the site permissions are set as inherit, the default permissions will be used.

Best practices

Some of the best practices are mentioned in the following sections.

Create a group for admins

Managing administrators is easier if you create a group for them. Although AD groups will not sync automatically, you can use `tabcmd` to automate setting permissions of this group. This will allow you to add and remove users from the admin role as needed.

Brainstorm security model

Gather a group of Tableau Desktop users and key stakeholders to discuss the typical use cases of permissions. Try and answer some of the following questions:

- Are we visualizing sensitive data that needs to be controlled via special sites?
- Who needs permissions to publish?
- Who needs permissions to edit other users' dashboards?
- What viewer roles do we have? Are all viewers the same regarding permissions?
- What projects will be required? How will publishing and viewing be different for every project?
- Are there any people who will always have a role regardless of the project?

Inheriting permissions

If you're going to use the Inherit permission option, it is better to have a plan. Inherit can get very confusing if you don't know what's being inherited. Here are some tips:

 Use the `Default` project as a template because all new projects will inherit permissions from the default project. Here are a few options to do that:

- Option one is to make the default project restrictive and to explicitly deny all permissions. In this case, all new projects will Inherit the permission of deny from the default project.
- Option two is to make the default project interactive but read-only with no access to underlying data. By disabling `View Underlying Data` and `Download Workbook` for the default project, all new projects will Inherit these permissions.
- Option three is to remove `all users` from the `default` group. This means any new project created will not Inherit any permission from the default project.

Start simple

Create a group per role for some projects, and set the permissions for the groups in the project accordingly. Use a UAT period to test the permissions and review before launching a live project.

Avoid custom permissions

Try not to set custom permissions when publishing. If this is really needed, make a separate site.

Regular review

If you are an administrator, educate users about the permission model, and make sure new Tableau Desktop users are given a general introduction about their responsibilities in setting permissions. Make sure you review the permissions on a regular basis and get feedback from users and key stakeholders.

Summary

In summary, you should keep in mind the following best practices for data blending. You should remember the permission hierarchy: `data source permissions | workbook permissions | group permissions | project permissions | site permissions`. You should use the default project as a template because all new projects will inherit permissions from the default project. You should avoid custom permissions. You should educate users on permissions and review the permissions regularly.

10
New features in Tableau 10

In the previous chapter, we talked about how to set permissions. In this chapter, we will talk about the exciting new features in Tableau 10.

In this chapter, we will cover the following:

- More data connections
- Cross data set filter
- Geo grouping
- Cross database join
- Workbook formatting
- Device-specific design

More data connections

In Tableau, there are three new data connectors to Google Sheets, Kognitio, and QuickBooks Online, as shown in the following screenshot:

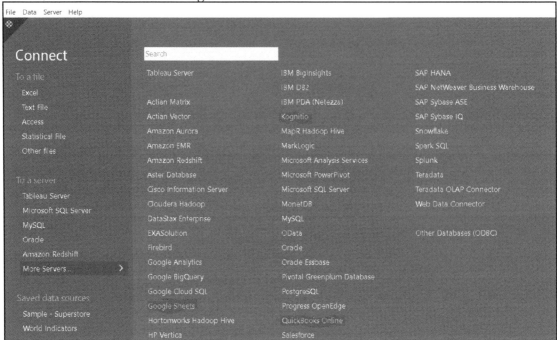

Cross data set filter

Before Tableau 10, you could use a field as a filter only if it was in the data set. If you had multiple fields in different data sets that are the kind of the same, for example, date or state, you would want to have one date or state filter for all the data sets. The old trick was to create a parameter and then create calculated fields using the same parameter for each dataset, and use the calculated fields as filters.

In Tableau 10, you will be able to apply the quick filter to all related sources, as shown next:

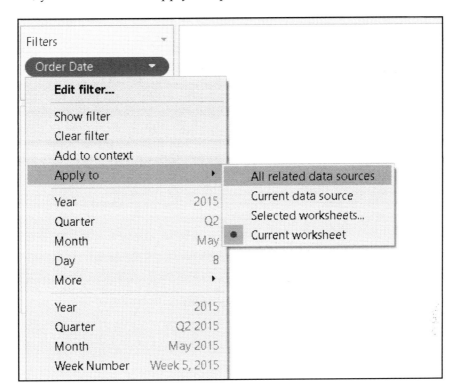

However, if the fields in your data sets are not named exactly the same, for example, Zip versus Zip Code, you will need to go to **Data | Edit Relationships** to build the relationship of those two fields.

Geo group

Sometimes you want to create group for your geolocation. For example, you many have states in your dataset, but you want to group the states into your sales territories, such as West, East, South, and North. In Tableau 10, you can easily create geo groups in your view.

Use your mouse to select the areas you want to group together:

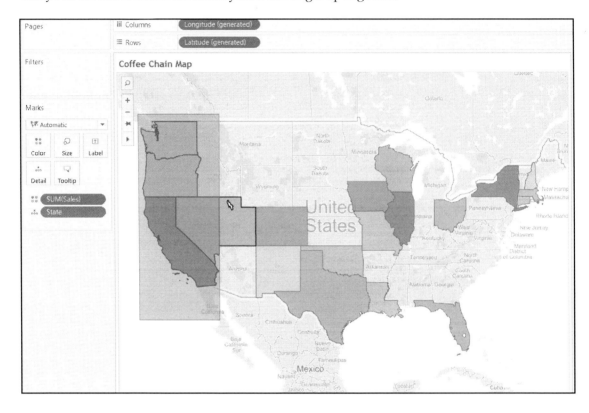

Click on the group icon to create the group:

Now you have created a geo group:

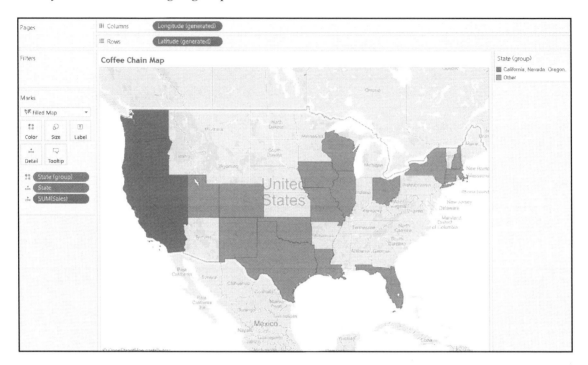

Cross database join

This is probably the most exciting new feature in Tableau 10. I am sure you all have the experience of using data blending to bring data from different sources together and trying to figure out all the limitations of primary vs secondary data sources. Not any more!

With cross database join, we can simply combine two data sets and analyze the total sales, as shown in the following screenshot:

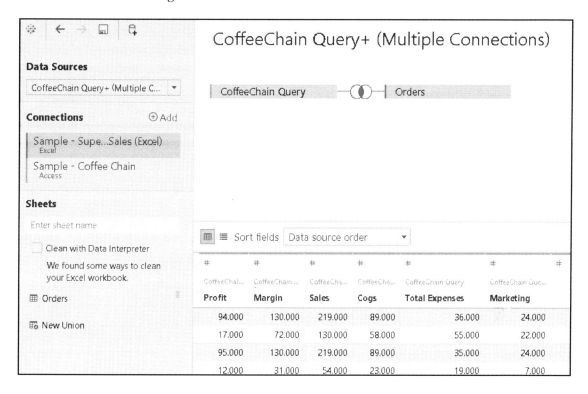

Workbook formatting

In Tableau 10, you can easily change the format of your entire workbook using the **Workbook** feature under `Format`:

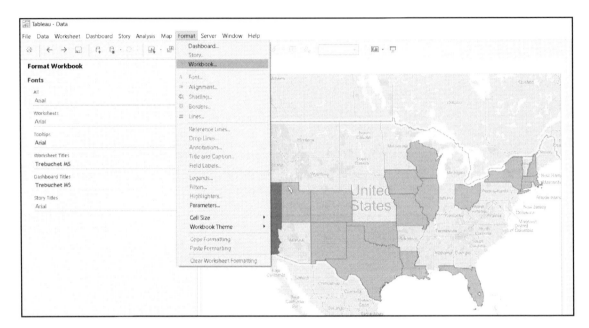

Device specific design

We all live in this multi-screen era, and we all know that bringing the best data visualization experience to mobile can be very challenging due to the nature of small screen.

In Tableau 10, you can easily customize your view to optimize it for the mobile experience.

To customize your view, click on **Show Preview**:

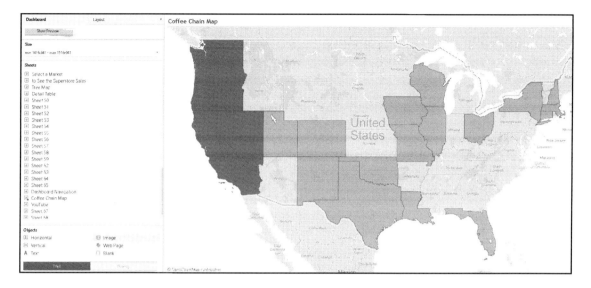

You can change the device type and model to see what your view looks like in each device, and customize your view accordingly:

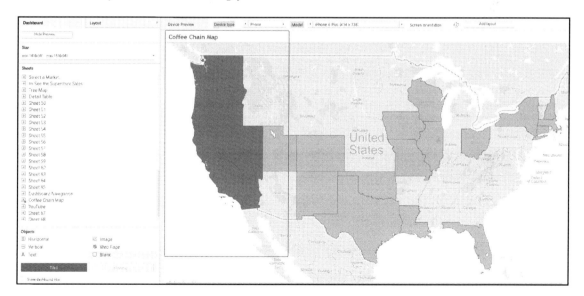

Summary

In summary, there are many exciting new features in Tableau 10. You can do cross database join and cross data set filter. You can do custom geo grouping. You can format the entire workbook. You can design device specific dashboards.

Index

Made in the USA
Columbia, SC
23 September 2018